LIGHT AFTER DARKNESS

Exiles: Charles and James Juchau

Roger Juchau

Table of Contents

List of Exhibits:

Preface

This book is an account of two men, Charles Juchau, a French Huguenot from Poitou, and his great grandson James Juchau, an Englishman born in London. Both made new lives in new homelands after having left their country of birth. There were elements of compulsion which brought about their leaving – one to largely escape religious persecution, the other forced because of a criminal conviction. Both men were of Huguenot descent – one immediate, the other distant.

Their stories add to the growing literature describing and explaining the migratory, refugee and settlement experience as well as furthering insight into the life of Huguenots and their descendants in France and elsewhere. They went from exclusion to inclusion. The psychological pressures they experienced during the departure, transit and arrival, and the ultimate process of settlement can only be surmised, since no records exist of their personal journeys. They both settled and raised families in new homelands, Charles in England and James in colonial NSW.

This book gives an understanding of the settings of their lives and origins, and the events which brought change and challenge. Where possible their responses are outlined, as well drawing on other literature to give an explanation of what they experienced in the upheaval of relocation, their journeys and the building of new lives. It explores and examines how two lives became woven into new societies. It responds to the appeal by many historians for more personal studies, focussing on the fate of individuals in important historical transitions – in this case, a Huguenot refugee and a convict transportee. The accounts bridge the two halves of both the Huguenot and the convict experiences.

The book draws on a range of resources including those which are listed in the acknowledgements. Conventional referencing of sources and acknowledgements are not used. There is some reservation about some Poitou Protestant and convict histories. They rely on a limited archive, including those personal accounts by other Huguenot refugees and transported convicts. Many writers have warned that these personal accounts suffer from the impediments of both reconstruction and selectivity.

The French region, Poitou, is an historic region which comprised the departments of Deux Sèvres, Vienne, and Vendée. New regional groupings were formed in the 1950s. Vendée (capital – La Roche Sur Yon) is now part of the Pays De La Loire region and Deux Sèvres (capital – Niort) and Vienne (capital – Poitiers) are now part of the Poitou-Charentes region. Historically, Poitou had a strong Calvinist following and spread from Luçon in the west to Poitiers in the east. At the centre was Fontenay-le-Comte. In reference to the trident and Calvinism, these three towns were represented as *un centre de la Reforme Tridentine*. In the text, the descriptions Calvinist, Protestant, and Huguenot, are interchanged when referring to members of the French Reformed Church, which was guided by the teachings of Calvin.

The surname Juchau and its spelling need clarification. From the website, www.geopatronyme.com, the name, Juchault, was centred in the old Province of Poitou in western France. The name Juchau is derived from Juchault. This name and its variants are still found in the three departments, Vienne, Vendée and Deux-Sèvres. The name was subject to a range of spellings in official records and in church baptismal, marriage and burial entries. The variations were an outcome of low literacy conditions. In England the name Juchau also acquired different spellings. In France it was sometimes spelt Juchaux, Juchaud, and Jucheau. All forms were found in the archives of Deux-Sèvres as early as the 17th century. Today they appear in the current phone directories of the three departments. Juchault is the dominant entry.

A Protestant archive centre at La Couarde, near Beaussais, and the departmental archive at Niort contain archival material on some Calvinist births, marriages and burials as well as lists of those who abjured and those who fled abroad. Entries go back to the mid1600s. Many entries for Juchault and variants are located there with only one for the departing Charles. Both in England and colonial NSW the spelling continued to be subject to transcribing and deciphering errors. Spelling errors included Juchan, Jucha, Inchau, Uchan and Incham. In Australia, USA and South Africa today the name is universally spelt Juchau.

There is an extensive literature on refugees and forced migration which seeks to capture the dynamics and effects of exclusion, movement, settlement, and encounter. To the extent it is possible from sources used, this account is about encounter, which shows that the human spirit can flourish and a fruitful life is always possible. Charles and James, forced out of their native countries, were both newcomers and undertook to build new lives. In their cases their encounters reveal a relatively successful transplantation. They moved from exclusion to inclusion.

Light after darkness was the experience of our two characters, Charles and James. Out of difficulty and disadvantage they emerged to win new and successful lives in new homelands.

CHAPTER 1
Introduction

Charles Juchault and James Juchau both experienced exile. Just over a hundred years separated their exile – Charles from France to England around 1710 and James from England to Australia in 1830. Charles was James' great grandfather.

Charles, a Calvinist, and lay preacher, found life difficult in Catholic France and he and another family member, Louis Juchault, sought a new life by fleeing to England. Records in England had Juchault more commonly spelt Juchau. James, a juvenile felon, was transported from England to Australia, where he was assigned to seven years of convict life in the penal settlement of Sydney. One sought refuge and freedom and the other was transported overseas to a period of captivity. As young men they both shared the experience of a new country and of navigating lives in testing and alien conditions.

They encountered the challenges of exit and entry and the anxieties of departure and arrival. Both could no longer stay in their country of birth and travelled to new homelands with no parental support. They encountered the psychological trauma of displacement. Contending with strangers and novel environments made demands on their capacities to adapt and survive. Charles had the benefit of an expatriate community to cushion his arrival, whilst James had no community to offset arrival anxieties and ease the shocks of displacement. Their backgrounds gave them strength to successfully pursue a fresh life.

Their lives prior to exile were very different.

Charles was raised in rural France in La Mothe St. Héray in the Deux-Sèvres department of the Poitou region of south west France. His birth date is unknown, but it is likely he was born around 1690. His family were Calvinists (referred also as either French Protestants or Huguenots) surviving difficult social, economic and political conditions. They faced persecution and endured the repression of Protestant religious and social practices, set up under the policies of Louis XIV who was trying to eliminate Protestantism from France. His Juchault forbears would have experienced the French Wars of Religion (1562-1629) which impacted Poitou.

Many Poitevins (inhabitants of Poitou) had left France during these wars, especially after 1572 (Massacre of St Bartholomew). From the 1670s Charles' family and his community would have suffered as Louis XIV (1643-1715) removed the political and religious freedoms of Calvinists. Between 1670 and 1715 large numbers of Huguenots left France for destinations offering more favourable economic, political and religious conditions. The motivation to leave was for social and economic reasons. As a recent observer noted, emigrating Poitevins were a mix of religious refugees and labour migrants. In the main, they headed for the Netherlands, Germany, Ireland, England, North America and South Africa. Charles took part in this exodus.

Around a century later, James was born in 1814 into a large working class family in London's East End, where poverty and squalor were experienced by many of the inhabitants in this part of London. Most families there faced hardship and misery. James received little or no education and had to assist his family by working as a gardener and errand boy. Prospects were grim in an area where unemployment and population growth gave little hope. The opportunity for a prosperous and healthy life was not in the offing for poor, unskilled, large working class families in the East End. Children had to fend as best they could and, for many, crime offered the only way to obtain money to alleviate poverty and to support their family. It appears that James followed this path. He was arrested for stealing and sentenced to transportation to the colony of NSW where he arrived in 1830.

They were cast into different lands and into quite different communities.

Charles came to Georgian England sometime in the 1709-11 period, accompanied by a relative Louis. Historical records show that when he left France his surname was recorded as Juchault. He found his way to a closely settled and working class community in the Soho area of London. He was entering a transforming and expanding London. He was part of the Huguenot exodus, aspects of which brought economic and cultural transformation to parts of 17th and 18th century Europe. In London he faced congested housing, expanding commerce and growing industry, all of these impacted by rapid population growth, boosted by rural and immigrant families seeking new lives. He was faced with another language, new customs and a crowded urban environment.

On arriving in England, Charles encountered many of his Calvinist countrymen, who also had migrated to London, settling in either the east around Spitalfields or to the west around Soho and Leicester Fields. His adjustment to a new life may have been tempered by French networks and institutions, built up over a hundred years of French Calvinist migration to London. Earlier arrivals from his home region also may have eased the adjustment burden, by offering contacts and settlement intelligence. London was now his home. He had to build a life, raise a family and realise there was no turning back to France, where persecution and tough economic conditions continued unabated. An Englishman he would be.

James arrived in colonial NSW with no knowledge of how and where his period of sentence was to be served. He came ashore in Sydney, where town and civic life fought to put aside its penal overtone. The emerging permanent buildings and roadways, the arrival of free settlers and the stirrings of commercial life might have given him a hint that Sydney was heading for prosperity. The uncertainty of his immediate destiny was quickly removed when he found himself in Carters' Barracks with other juvenile male convicts. He was directed into an apprenticeship to learn harness making. His social milieu included adult and juvenile convicts, soldiers, instructors and occasional contacts with townspeople.

Glimpses of natural Sydney and local aborigines gave prospect of an exotic country offering perhaps a new life after serving time. Any outlook for his future may have been limited by information on his options, including a return to England, or a new independent life in the colony, or continuing to work in the colony as hired labour. And whatever options were considered, he would have been handicapped by his background and little education. He would not know that he would eventually be a free man and successful colonialist in rural NSW.

Charles and James both experienced different times of Hanoverian London, where the progress of the Industrial Revolution and the impacts of a growing and changing British Empire were evident. They also experienced the rule of constitutional monarchs: Charles under George I and George II; James under George III and George IV. They both observed the consequences of various English wars and disputes with its continental neighbours. They both experienced a London in transformation and growth.

They both shared the experience of spending their lives in two countries. It is not known how much of their first homeland experiences and values were carried over to their new homelands. Charles spent around 20 years in France and around 45 years in England. James spent 15 years in England and 67 years in NSW. Time spent in each country would influence their outlook and values. Charles encountered a strikingly different culture and place of residence and James, while experiencing vestiges of English culture, encountered an abrupt change in environment and an emerging culture, shaped by fresh views about opportunity and advancement. At the end of their lives, when drawing up their personal inventories of life, they could easily have concluded that the second parts of their lives were positive periods which far outweighed the negative aspects of the first parts of their lives.

Map 17th Century France

Calais

Cambrai

Le Havre

Amiens • Péronne

Rouen PICARDY

Rheims

NORMANDY

Evreux • Mantes Meaux

Strasbourg

St Germain-en-Laye

Paris

Châlons-sur-Marne

BRITTANY

Alençon • Verneuil • Dreux Vincennes

Rennes •

Étampes •

CHAMPAGNE

Le Mans • Châteaudun Fontainebleau • Sens

ANJOU

Orléans • Auxerre

R. Seine

Angers •

Tours Blois

R. Loire

Saumur

Amboise

Nantes

Châtellerault • Bourges • La Charité Dijon

POITOU

Poitiers • BERRY Nevers

Châteauroux BURGUNDY

La Rochelle

R. Charente MARCHE

R. Saône

Mâcon

Geneva

Angoulême

Lyon

ANGOUMOIS

Issoire • Vienne

Bordeaux R. Dordogne Bergerac

Grenoble

R. Rhône Valence

Cahors

R. Lot Mende DAUPHINE

GUYENNE

Nérac • Agen Montauban Orange

R. Tarn

Bayonne

Toulouse Nîmes Avignon

BÉARN

LANGUEDOC

Montpellier • PROVENCE

Garonne

Béziers Aix-en-Provence

Carcassonne

R.

10

CHAPTER 2
Calvinists and Poitou

Until the French Revolution, the Poitou area was subject to a monarchic and political system referred to as the Ancient Regime. It was a feudal, social and political order centred on the king and noble families. Over the 16th, 17th and 18th centuries there was a drive by French monarchs to secure political centralisation over the scattered political and economic centres of France. The drive to centralise and to boost tax revenue generated resentment and revolts in the regions, including rural households and noble families, who disputed and resented the monarch's intrusions. The Wars of Religion coincided with these endeavours, but once concluded, the centralisation was further intensified, especially under Louis XIV and his Secretary of State for war, Louvois.

Louis XIV regarded France's "bi-confessionalism" as an obstacle to absolute rule. He also considered religious freedom as a threat to unity in his kingdom. Louis waged a campaign to eradicate Calvinism and this was aided by one of his key centralising measures, the appointment of *Intendants* who were the king's provincial representatives and who undermined the power of local nobles. Their powers included taxing on behalf of the King and enforcing his laws and anti – Calvinist directives. These directives included the forced coercion and conversion of Calvinists to Catholicism and a range of punitive measures against those evading conversion. Their actions brought upheaval and disruption to the lives of Poitou's Calvinists in both the 17th and 18th centuries.

The king had a repertoire of coercive measures drawn from the experience of handling popular revolts. Included in this repertoire was the lodging of troops in households. Lodgement of troops was a strategy widely used to deal with uprisings and revolts. The troops made harsh physical and financial demands designed to corral, humble and punish rebelling populations. The quartering of troops also reduced costs of army provisioning and the policing of communities. Troop lodgements were widely used in Poitou to enforce conversion.

At the beginning of the 17th century it has been estimated that of France's population of 15 million around eight to ten percent were Protestants. Adherents to Calvinism were found in many areas of France but around three quarters of them were located south of the Loire, especially in the three regions where the eradication campaigns became strongly focussed – Poitou, Béarn and Languedoc, especially Bas -Languedoc. Cities in the south became Protestant strongholds and included La Rochelle, Castres, Montauban, and Nîmes.

By 1780, the campaigns had largely removed Calvinism from Béarn; in Poitou it had reduced Calvinists by 60 percent, while in some parts of Languedoc only a decline of five percent was registered. Conversions to the Catholic faith and emigration accounted for these losses. Some claims indicated that in 1685 the Protestant population had fallen to 800,000. Over the period 1680-1780 it was estimated that around 200,000 had left France constituting one of the largest migration waves in early modern European history.

Reliable accounts of 17th century Poitou rural and Protestant life and for most of the 18th century are limited. Like the rest of France's population 85 percent of Poitou inhabitants were rural dwellers, often clustered around hamlets and linked to provincial towns by tracks and pathways which were often in poor repair. If you were to believe Arthur Young, who travelled some of the region prior to the revolution in1787, some of the area was not well farmed and poverty was apparent in many settlements. He reported that in parts, it was an unimproved, poor and ugly country. He noted uncultivated tracts of land and families living in hovels. In Vendée he observed wasteland, brushwood, heath and morass with some cultivation of rye and buckwheat. Interspersed across the area were walled-in houses and farmsteads. The principal road of the region linked Nantes to La Rochelle.

The old Poitou province had three departments, Vendée, Vienne and Deux-Sèvres where, in the 16th century, Calvinism took root and by 1670, had around 80,000 followers. The departments varied in the number of followers. Vendée (Bas – Poitou) had around 20,000 followers, Vienne (Haut – Poitou) 15,000, and Deux-Sèvres (Moyen – Poitou) 45,000. The Calvinists, referred to as *les églises réformées*, operated through synods which served the three departments. In Poitou, the Calvinist community were referred to in French as *la communauté réformée poitevine.*

The data on Calvinist numbers are unreliable. Some sources had Vendée numbers closer to those of Deux-Sèvres. At the peak of Calvinism in the 16th century, it was claimed that Vendée had 36,000 followers – 2000 fewer than Deux – Sèvres. Vienne always registered fewer followers across the three centuries of wars and persecutions. Over these three centuries, the location of Protestant activism became more rural and less urban.

Deux-Sèvres, an agricultural area with fertile soils, streams and forests, was viewed by authorities as ultimately having the highest concentration of Calvinists in Poitou.

Historically, this department was bounded by Vouille in the west, Saint Maixent l'Ecole in the north, Vançais in the east and Melle in the south. To the north were the old provinces of Anjou, Brittany and Touraine, to the east Berry, Limousin and Marche, to the south Aunis Saintonge and Angoumois and, to the west, the Atlantic Ocean. Calvinist activity was well supported in the centres of Niort, Saint Maixent l'Ecole, Melle and Mougon.

In the 16th century, rural families and townspeople of Poitou, often encouraged and led by local noble families, had embraced Calvinism. Among other things, its style and confessional practices were attractive because it gave scope for a more independent, progressive life and met the aspirations of a community seeking more freedom from the imposts of Catholic France. Calvinists were often referred to as *réligionairres*

During the 16th and 17th centuries Poitou experienced the French Wars of Religion (1562-1629). The wars disrupted community cohesion and food production, placing great pressures on the economy and the social order of the region. Poitou felt the ravages of these wars as Catholic and Protestant armies criss-crossed the region. Individuals and groups from Poitou emigrated to escape the effects of these wars. One group found their way to Nova Scotia, Canada in 1604.

The wars brought suffering and losses to the community. The fighting led to church and building destruction in communities including Niort, Poitiers, Melle, St Maixent L'Ecole (St Maixent) and La Mothe-St-Héray. The last town was originally two communes La Mothe, where there was a destroyed castle, and Saint Héray, where there was an ancient church. In more recent times, it has become one community and it is referred to as La Mothe when referenced here and in some Poitou literature.

All these communities had to contend with the wars for nearly 60 years. They dealt with difficulties and managed to hold households together despite friction, division, economic losses and turmoil. And despite the Edict of Nantes in 1598, which promised freedom and peace to Protestants, friction and upheaval remained, only to grow again in the second half of the 17th century, as the Catholic monarchs took action to remove Protestant presence in France.

The major port servicing the Poitou region and the principal centre of Protestant resistance, La Rochelle, felt the brunt of these actions. Catholic armies finally crushed Protestant resistance there in 1629. Within three decades more turmoil and suffering was to emerge as the monarch pressed to remove Protestantism from France.

While the advent of Calvinism had brought new freedoms to Poitou it also promoted hostile reaction from ruling Catholic groups, leading to a situation where for nearly three centuries, the Calvinists endured wars and persecution. While they were not the only religious minority in Europe to face opposition, they were somewhat unique in the geographic distribution of the social, economic and political upheaval experienced. Their destiny was to become a persecuted minority. Yet again, as history has shown, many of this persecuted minority were driven to seek better and safer lives elsewhere.

Besides persecution and repression, Calvinists had to endure, along with the rest of the population, the economic consequences of adverse climate conditions, especially the severe winters. The fortunes of Poitou, with the rest of rural France, were subject to climatic rhythms impacting on the quality and quantity of harvests, which in turn governed the material life of families. A bad harvest was felt by all. Winter conditions often hit France hard. For example, in 1708-9, France experienced a devastating winter, the coldest for 500 years. Famine and destitution resulted and, like most of France, Poitou suffered badly. It was recorded as the last great famine in the history of France.

Because ordinary family and household experiences of Poitou Protestants during the Calvinist period are not extensively documented, the portrayal of events has had to rely on fragmentary evidence and unsystematic records of Calvinist activities. As well, many accounts of events, often compiled and mediated by exiled Calvinist ministers, included memoires which were exaggerated to highlight Catholic cruelty and repression. Some of these did not give a complete story of the friendly co-existence between faiths. It has been noted that cross-confessional friendships and support were widely experienced in Poitou.

As social and political conditions changed over the 16th and 17th centuries, when rights to freely practice religion became increasingly difficult, formal Calvinist records diminished. Calvinists had to change their religious routines and, by 1690, Calvinist proceedings had become covert, and formal records of events were secreted away. This has limited the understanding of how events impacted on the lives of ordinary Poitevins.

The reaction of Poitevins to the King's anti-Calvinist campaign has been characterised as one of passive resistance and non-conformity. Amongst those Calvinists who converted, estimated at 38,000 in Poitou, abjuration was claimed to be "by mouth but not by the heart" or, as others have put it, "religion made no progress in their hearts". Others resisted and inwardly held on to their beliefs keeping their religion alive through stealth and cautiousness whenever open displays of worship occurred. There was reluctance to keep written records of personal and family affairs, for fear they could be used by authorities when carrying out the king's orders.

As already noted, building a definitive picture of the life of Protestants in Poitou is difficult, because of a limited and unreliable archive. Documents of officialdom, church, parish, and town records, together with the memoirs of church leaders and prominent families are the main sources. Protestant social life paralleled the lives of their Catholic neighbours where, in a largely rural community, they all experienced the vagaries of a rural economy and all were involved in farming and related rural and township trades. In Poitou, it was often the quality of farming practices and artisan skills which, together with religious commitments, distinguished Protestants from their Catholic neighbours.

Some observers of the Protestant population around the end of the 17th century also noted that there were differences in their occupations, habits and outlook. In Deux-Sèvres, Protestants tended to be running or working on farms whilst others lived in settlements as officials, merchants, artisans and professionals. Some observers noted that *Protestantism Poitevin* was essentially rural in character and marked by a spirit of independence.

Their agricultural and commercial successes, their involvement in profitable grain milling and their wider community contributions generated a view that Poitou Protestants exhibited greater industry, wealth and resourcefulness and were more open to new ideas. This was attributed, in part, to the higher level of literacy noted amongst many Protestant families. An open attitude and preparedness to accept progress was also noted. This gave the impression to some observers that individualism and learning were highly valued by Protestant families. More extreme claims had them being more independent, harder working, more enterprising and better informed than their Catholic neighbours, who were claimed to be burdened by lower levels of literacy and a conservative clergy.

Outside the limited schooling in certain locations provided by Jesuits, there was no formal provision of basic education for rural Catholics. Most rural people could neither read nor write. For ordinary Catholics, the local curés taught children to recite the catechism or spell a credo and paternoster. Amongst large segments of their population, the systematic teaching of reading, writing and arithmetic was largely neglected. The wealthy among Catholics and Protestants had tutors to teach basics and used private schooling. Protestant schools in Poitou were closed by mid 17th century forcing many Protestant households to teach the rudiments of reading and writing accompanied by instruction in Calvinist principles.

The qualities and skills of French Protestants gave them advantages which other countries welcomed, such as in the case of Prussia, which encouraged some 20,000 Huguenots to settle in Germany in the state of Brandenburg. They received, amongst other things, assisted housing and tax exemptions. Their industry and skills were used to support the rebuilding of the Prussian state, following the ravages of the Thirty Years Wars (1618-48).

Protestant groups throughout France maintained their resolve to uphold their beliefs in the face of increasing mistreatment and persecution. Calvinism gave them a pathway to obtain a more open and independent life and, coincidentally, a valuable social vehicle for people with common aspirations to band together. They sought greater freedom from the imperatives and dictates of the Catholic Church. They sought relief from the taxing regimes and controls of the monarch and his agents. In many regions it particularly appealed to the rising urban bourgeoisie and a cross section of the nobility.

As to why Poitou embraced and sustained Calvinism, when in nearby regions with similar social characteristics and economy, there were less enthusiastic responses to Calvinism, continues to be an intriguing question. Apart from a relatively intense exposure to Calvinist preaching and communication links with La Rochelle, one explanation may be that this community, because of its relatively active economy, rural solidarity, social cohesion and community leadership, embraced Calvinism as a means to build a better community, through spiritual and economic commitments. It assisted in furthering local identity and strengthening opposition to centralised power. And in this rural setting they had, for the most part, the advantage of long standing and friendly Catholic neighbours, most of whom saw little threat in the adoption and presence of a new faith in their midst.

Calvinists were comfortable about expressing opposition to injustice and unfairness, including the actions of the taxing authorities. And their capacity to embrace and sustain their faith, despite encountering wars and persecution, perhaps lies in their stoicism, social and community vitality, supported by favourable social conditions, rural geography and economy.

Poitou's topography consisted of France's Atlantic coastal plain, adjoined by an undulating hilly area and further to the east the first foothills of the Massif Central. The communities across the plain and plateau areas of Poitou enjoyed a diversified agriculture. Dominating part of the landscape was the *Bocage*, a terrain of mixed woodland and pasture, which was regarded as a defining feature of much of the region by many travellers. Some parts of Poitou were favoured by good soils, an accommodating terrain and moderate climate. While farming in the region could be

Map Protestant Concentration 17th Century Poitou

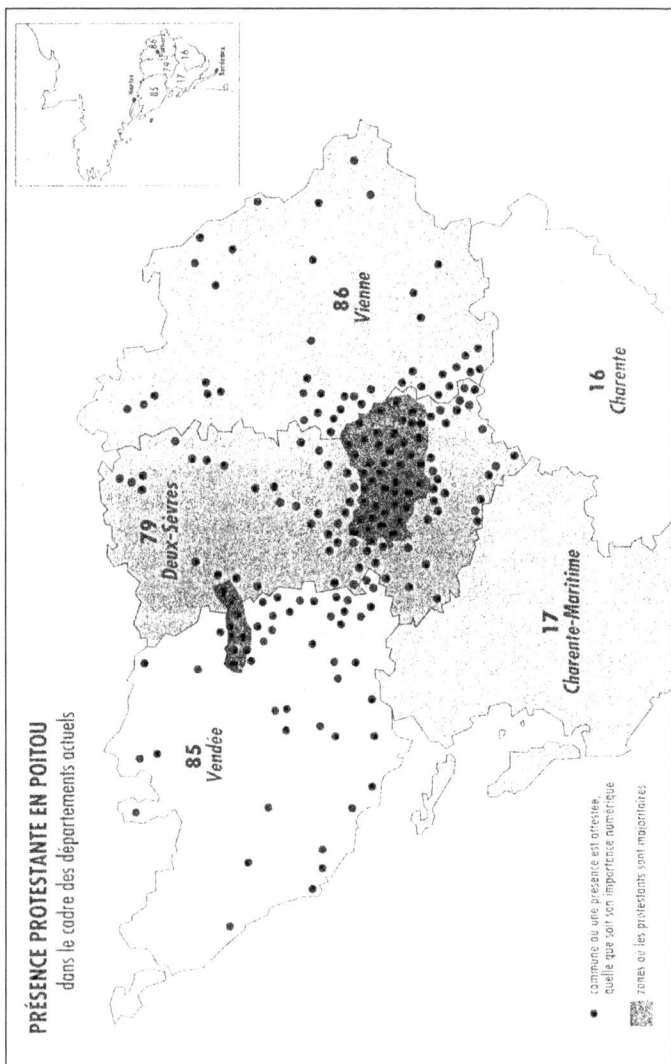

PRÉSENCE PROTESTANTE EN POITOU
dans le cadre des départements actuels

86 Vienne

16 Charente

79 Deux-Sèvres

17 Charente-Maritime

85 Vendée

- commune ou une présence est attestée,
quelle que soit son importance numérique

zones ou les protestants sont majoritaires

Source: J Marcade, P.13

challenging, it benefited from profitable animal and crop production. In Deux Sèvres for example, fertile soils, accessible water sources, and reliable river flows sustained both intensive and extensive agriculture and supported town life. Rivers were important for small river craft and for the water mills which produced large amounts of flour for export.

Farming generated steady incomes. Active markets in nearby towns facilitated the commerce of agriculture. The economy in many hamlets was supported by innkeepers, shoemakers, bakers, tailors, and stone masons. In larger settlements there were surgeons, apothecaries, doctors, lawyers and artisans. Cloth and fabric manufacturers, including weavers, tanners, dyers, and card makers, aided commerce in some of the towns of Poitou. Land holdings spanned small farms, larger estates of the landed gentry as well as the holdings of noble families. Farms often had tenants, including *metayers,* who worked the farms and shared the yields with the landowners. Taxes were levied on farm produce including taxes on animals raised on farms. On some farms taxes influenced animal husbandry practices.

Upland areas of Poitou, such as around Parthenay and Melle, supported large animal production through extensive pastures especially in the Gatine of Parthenay. Much of the plain (Plaine de Niort) produced grain crops such as corn, wheat, rye, barley and oats. Corn was a key staple and was also important for market trade. Sheep were important for meat and wool, and were supplemented by meat and by-products of cattle, pigs, poultry and goats. Horse and donkey breeding together with mules extended the economic base of farming. Mules were used as plough and pack animals as well as being an important source of export revenue to countries like Spain. Grasses, linseed and hemp were also harvested.

Crop rotation, manuring and fallow practices were widespread. Fodder crops, such as sainfoin, chickling and vetch were cultivated and often obtained higher prices than barley and oats in the markets. Fields were often enclosed by hedgerows. Throughout the region woodlands were present as well as chestnut and walnut groves. Forestry was important for wood supply and small quarries supplied stone for buildings, gardens, walls and paving.

As noted, many farm households clustered around small hamlets and larger farm estates were established by wealthy families. Household vegetable and small animal production, conducted in fenced hamlet plots, were also critical to the rural economy. Small farms, up to 10 hectares, were known as *borderie* and larger, up to 50 hectares, were known as *metairie*. Some land was leased successfully and tenant farmers had a reputation for being hard working and industrious. Common land and common pastures supported grazing. Regional centres, Melle, La Mothe, and St. Maixent, conducted regular markets and the associated trade anchored the wealth of the region. Rivers, rudimentary roads and pathways, important for trade and communication, linked villages to important major towns, principally Niort, Fontenay-le-Comte, La Rochelle and Poitiers.

Flour was a critical export and was sent to markets and ports via small barges, bullock carts and pack mules. A two-way traffic had emerged. Flour, produced at water mills, *moulins de la Sèvre,* such as those at La Mothe and Exoudun, was exported together with cloth, salted meat and leather, while salt, resin and salted fish were imported. The export of flour was very significant to the economy and the sacks or bumpkins of flour, known as *les minots du poitou* found their way to France's overseas possessions. Mules and donkeys were especially important for transporting goods and the area long enjoyed a good reputation for its mules and mule breeding. River ports at Niort and Marans and the Atlantic sea port of La Rochelle were critical for import trade and the exporting of regional produce. La Rochelle, as noted, was a key city for disseminating Calvinism as well as sustaining it during the Wars of Religion. Later it became an important exit point for Protestants fleeing abroad to escape persecution.

In parts, Poitou enjoyed both a profitable agriculture and an industrious Calvinist rural population who coped with disruption and adversity. It survived climatic disasters and its population weathered increased religious turmoil. While many Calvinists saw emigration as the way to manage the future, others continued their customary lives and devised ways to see through the challenges and difficulties. With their religious affairs, many yielded to the King's directives and converted. Others, through either subterfuge or seclusion, upheld their faith and formed a passive resistance movement.

Calvinism kept a presence in Poitou and this gave it the basis to grow after the political changes of 1789. It has been estimated that in one department, Deux – Sèvres, there were 30,000 Protestants at the start of the 19th century. One part of Poitou, Vendée, achieved a permanent place in French history because it was the centre of a civil war (1793-96), *Guerre de Vendée,* when Royalist and Catholic armies, originating in Vendée, rebelled against the Revolutionary forces. There were atrocities on both sides and large numbers of peasants and townspeople were killed and the countryside ravaged and ruined. Some Protestants joined their Catholic neighbours to fight with the Royalists, others with the revolutionaries, whilst others tried to stay neutral but could not escape the impacts of the conflicts. Those disposed to the Royalists may have been influenced by the Edict of Toleration of Louis XVI in 1787, which restored rights to Protestants including the rights to live freely and to practise their trades and professions from which they previously had been excluded.

Map Principal Localities Deux-Sevres

Xaintray
Champdeniers
Champeaux
St-Georges-de-Noisné
Chantecorps
Ménigoute
Béceleuf
Clavé
Fomperron
Surin
Germond
La Chapelle-Bâton
Faye-sur-Ardin
Rouvre
St-Christophe-du-Roc
Augé
Saivres
Exireuil
Coudray-Salbart
Cherveux
St-Maixent-l'École
St-Maxire
Fonverrines
Azay-le-Brulé
Nanteuil
Pamproux
Échiré
Boisragon
St-Martin-de-St-Maixent
Ste-Eanne
St-Gelais
François
Ste-Néomaye
Salles
Chauray
Breloux
Aiript
Souvigné
La Mothe-St-Héray
Ruffigny
La Crèche
Roman
Souché
Chavagné
Aigonnay
Prailles
La Couarde
Exoudun
Vouillé
Bessines
NIORT
Fressines
Ch
Aiffres
Mougon
Thorigné
Beaussais
Chey
Vitré
Conzais
Celles-sur-Belle
Prahecq
Tauché
La Martinière
Le
Ste-Blandine
Verrines-sous-Celle
St-Martin-de-Bernegoue
St-Médard
St-Martin
Melle
St-Roman-les-Melle
St-Léger-la-Martinière
Montigné
Brûlain
Mazière-sur-Beffronne
Maisonnay
Beauvoir-sur-Niort
Secondigné-sur-Belle
Paizay-le-Tort
Vernoux-sur-Boutonne
Forêt de Chizé
Lusseray
Tillou
Brioux-sur-Boutonne
Luché-sur-Brioux
Chizé
Fontenille
Chérigné
St-Martin-d'Entraigues
Chef-Bouto
Dampierre-sur-Boutonne
Paizay-le-Chapt

CHAPTER 3
Charles, Calvinism and Poitou

Charles and many Juchault families came from the Deux-Sèvres department and were involved in some way with agriculture. Other Juchaults lived in neighbouring Vendée and Vienne. No clear French records exist about Charles, his place of birth, his family or other personal data. One Protestant family archive entry records Charles leaving Deux Sèvres as part of the Huguenot exodus, possibly sometime in the period 1709-11. This French record shows that he and a relative, Louis, both from La Mothe St. Héray, left for London and that Charles was a lay preacher. In this record their names were spelt Juchault.

Based on his English marriage and death records it was probable that he was born around 1690 and was around twenty when he left France. This record indicated that he subsequently married in London. It was likely he was a rural dweller, possessing little formal education, few resources and was unsettled by the persecution. His community was under stress and the oppression experienced throughout his early life may have turned his thoughts to leave his community. Most of his resources would have been used in financing his passage through France and then on to England.

Present and recorded distributions of the Juchault name and variants of the name suggest that his extended family would had lived in one of the rural communities of Deux-Sèvres, in or around such villages as Prailles, Beaussais, Exoudun, Melle or La Mothe, all of which today still have an economic dependency on agriculture. Like the rest of the community, he probably came from a large family.

Typically a married Protestant couple in rural Poitou had at least five children. The department lies between two rivers, la Sèvre Nantaise which flows into the sea at Nantes and la Sèvre Niortaise which flows into the sea at Niort, hence the department name Deux (two) – Sèvres. The area contained key rural parishes where Protestants had become increasingly concentrated by the early 18th century.

As in many areas of France, the Juchault households and their forbears would have observed and experienced civil strife and tension following the Reformation. The French Wars of Religion and the accompanying civic strife impacted the affairs of early Juchaults. Later, Charles and his family would have felt the actions of Louis XIV trying to eliminate Protestantism from their communities. Religious, political and communal turmoil was encountered throughout the 16th, 17th and 18th centuries. In each century, religious and economic exile gathered momentum as the hostilities, oppression and unfavourable economic conditions persisted. Many Poitevins chose England as their place of refuge.

In Charles' community, two groups, the majority Catholic and the minority Protestant, which included most Juchault families, jointly felt this turmoil. Amongst other things Calvinists had to safeguard and uphold their idea of a communal life shaped by their religious beliefs. Fortunately it appears that in their rural communities and among ordinary people there was tolerance of faith differences. Social harmony obtained amongst most ordinary people. And for a period there was civil toleration of their religion.

The villages, where the Juchaults were concentrated, had this social harmony threatened once the monarch's decrees and actions to rid France of Calvinists became more severe and, as a result, disrupted social and economic affairs. For example some disharmony was experienced when, in a number of neighbourhoods, some Catholics heeded the king's directives and became willing informants, prepared to denounce their Protestant neighbours.

It was inevitable that dominant Catholic political interests, together with the French monarchy, were going to prevail through political and military power. Across France armed intervention, public protests and resistance movements could not prevent the crushing of Protestant rights and freedoms and the destruction of Protestant temples. The Juchaults, together with other Protestants across France, would have faced the challenge of holding onto their religious identity. Despite the hostile conditions they did not abandon local values shared with Catholic neighbours. They adhered to local folk beliefs and cultural practices. In Poitou daily lives and customary events were closely entwined and there was widespread sharing of festivities and celebrations.

Historical links to Catholicism and the overwhelming commitment of most French citizens to Catholicism meant that survival of the Protestant faith was always precariously balanced and struggled for permanency. It only commenced to regain a permanent and an unfettered footing in Poitou after 1789 when France entered a major period of political change including the rule of Napoleon. After 1802 Protestants in Poitou began to rebuild or reclaim temples and to once again freely prosecute their faith. In Beaussais, for example, a Catholic church was turned into a Protestant temple. Calvinism, or the Reformed Church, as it was also known, continued to hold a presence in France and recently, in 2012 joined with the Lutheran Church to form one Protestant organisation for France, now known as *L'Eglise Protestante Unie De France*. The single body has claimed that unity has not compromised the diversity and pluralism of French Protestant practices.

By 1680, the Calvinist population in Poitou had reached around 80,000 and was served by 52 pastors. When the king's anti-Calvinist directives took effect from around this date, the Protestant population of Poitou was set to decline through emigration and the forced conversion to Catholicism. In many of the Juchault households, much debate and agonising must have occurred in deciding whether to convert, leave or preserve their faith through covert activity. Until then, their religious involvements had suffered no direct threat. While they endured the destruction, tensions and effects of the Wars of Religion they had been able to hold on to their religion.

For the Juchault families, the first flowering of the Reformation in France came to their region when, in 1534, Calvin came from Picardy to Poitiers to preach. He advocated the translating of the bible from Latin into the local language so that his followers could have direct access to the word of God. Bible reading became the prime duty of every conscientious Protestant.

He was regarded as being more radical than Martin Luther. Calvin, through his theological ideas, his travels and his writing, established, arguably, the most widely influential branch of Protestantism. His preaching spurred his followers to read the bible and encouraged literacy as well revealing new ways to follow and uphold their religion. A special store on eduction and literacy meant that many Protestant communities soon surpassed the level of general literacy amongst their Catholic neighbours. His movement succeeded in accelerating the splitting of Christendom into three: Orthodox, Catholic and Protestant.

Large numbers of the followers of Calvin emerged in Vendée, Deux-Sèvres and Vienne, and by the 1550s, reformed churches (temples) began to appear in towns and rural communities.

The growth of Protestantism in Poitou was stimulated by the arrival of pastors from Geneva. In some respects, Protestantism's cause benefited from the dysfunction of the monarchs, in particular their political vacillation and ineffectiveness in the 1550-1595 period, when French rulers were unable to impose strict adherence to the Gallic principle of "one faith, one king, one law". Despite a strong Catholic presence, Protestantism found a receptive audience amongst Poitevins. Protestantism attracted the exploited and the oppressed, the literate and the successful. It included independent middle classes and a cross section of rural households. Rural families, like the Juchaults, were strongly represented as well as noble families.

Regular commerce and trade with the Atlantic port of La Rochelle, a strong centre of Calvinism, helped spread Calvinist ideas into southern Poitou, and in particular the department of Deux-Sèvres. In their rural and farming community the Juchaults and their neighbours would have interacted with the traders and merchants linked with La Rochelle. These links gave other perspectives of Calvinism and of its appeal to those seeking a faith which encouraged independence. Both the preaching and trade contacts assisted local Calvinism to flourish.

This Calvinist flowering, however, was set back once the royal military anti-protestant campaigns of Louis XIII(1610-43) and Louis XIV (1643-1715), known as the Sun-King, took hold. They hampered and curtailed Huguenot assemblies and activities and as well, they regained control of Huguenot territory lost during the Wars of Religion. The striving for a religious monocracy was evident and came to full realisation between 1661 to 1715 under Louis XIV's reign.

The first sign of these campaigns for Poitevins was when Louis XIII's armies defeated a Protestant army in 1622 in the marshes of Poitou (*le Marais Poitevin*). This was part of Louis XIII's successful campaign to put down Huguenot rebellions in South West France during the years 1621 to 1629. Guided by his Chief Minister of State, Cardinal Richelieu, he succeeded in removing the political, territorial and military rights of the Huguenots. He saw the decline of Protestant resistance and the royal recovery of the towns of Poitou which had been lost during the Wars of Religion. This was to herald a wave of further actions to remove Calvinist practices from France.

Louis XIV, driven in part by the imperative of the unity of church, king and country, stepped up action against Calvinism and in the 1660s he begun to set up various means to eliminate its presence from France. Beginning in Poitou, and soon extending throughout France, directives were issued to coerce the Protestants to convert. Poitevins were to experience terror and distress. He was aided by advisers, especially Louvois who, as a member of the king's council, directed operations and controlled the *Intendants*.

The King moved from passive and petty discrimination to aggressive persecution. The Juchaults, like others in Protestant communities, were to suffer oppression, dispossession and discrimination as the king moved to assure the primacy of French Catholic interests. He was to offer financial incentives to reward conversion as well as instituting military measures, to extirpate Protestantism by force.

In 1685, the king finally formally revoked, at the urging of powerful clerical interests, the protestant religious freedoms and practices which were gained in 1598 through the *Edict of Nantes* issued by Henry IV. It is claimed the revocation by Louis was partly motivated by royal paranoia and insecurity. Observers considered that the action of 1685 was the most dishonourable part of Louis XIV's long reign. One of the effects of the Revocation, the "decalvinisation" of France, led to many Calvinists of Poitou to evade the king's directives either by going abroad or upholding their religion through various covert means.

In Poitou, however, the Revocation spurred on a resurgence of Calvinism. One result was the development of networks of followers and a more resolute community of believers. Many have observed that the Revocation reinvigorated Calvinism in France, which had up to then shown signs of becoming moribund. It rekindled Huguenot spirit and determination. Through emigration, it also led to the spread of Calvinism to the New World where Calvinists established their communities to bring new skills in agricultural practices and cloth manufacturing. While these ventures appeared promising, observers noted that while these New World Huguenot enclaves had an economic base, they ultimately dissipated and filtered into their host communities. Most did not realise their dreams and became part of an integrated community, contributing to the betterment of their new homeland and host territory.

In the latter half of the 16th century the Protestant Poitevins, apart from the effects of the ravages of the religious wars, experienced poor harvests, food scarcity, taxes and levies, all of which contributed to economic distress in town and rural communities. And the king's military repression campaigns that followed in the 17th century brought no respite to this distress. The cumulative effects of the early religious wars and the repressive campaigns by the monarch brought continuing hardship to farm and peasant communities, although some artisan groups in larger settlements felt the hardship less. The economic dislocation and upheaval would have been felt by the Juchaults and meant that men in the community often deferred marriage until their affairs became more settled.

Poitou had experienced the decalvinising campaign well before the Revocation in 1685. In Poitou, as noted, the first signs of suppressing Protestant practices followed the final routing of the Protestant armies and the recovery of Protestant strongholds. The community was soon to see the start of a concerted campaign to restore Catholic dominance and coerce Protestants to abandon their faith. In one sense, the absolute authority of the monarchy was being imposed to restore order following the disorder of the Wars of Religion.

Poitou, like the rest of France, must have quickly realised that their monarch, Louis XIV, was hell bent on creating an ordered society and a society of orders. He was going to ensure that, as an officer of God, his Catholic religion would prevail at all costs. He believed he was the great defender and benefactor of the Catholic faith. During Louis XIV's reign, other Catholic princes in Europe also sought to curb the rights of Protestants and used persecution to remove dissenters from their realms.

The actions of Louis XIV inevitably generated social tensions and divisions. They firmed the resolve of many Protestants either to quietly resist conversion in some way or to flee and seek refuge abroad. During the Wars of Religion, Protestants from Poitou had previously sought refuge abroad. It was claimed that they were part of an early wave of refugees seeking asylum in Elizabethan London. Some parents also sent their children to safety abroad, often to live with relatives and often under the pretext of receiving education in another language.

A number of Juchaults came from around the communities of Thorigne and Prailles and would have heard of the Calvinist, Jean Migault, a local miller, notary and bible teacher from Mougon, a strong Calvinist community. He gained some notoriety for his refusal to convert, despite pressure on his family and the destruction of his house. He recorded in a journal, *Journal De Jean Migault (1682-1689)*, the persecutions of his family which had started in 1682. He refused to convert at first but, to save his large family of 14 children, he finally abjured while in prison in La Rochelle. Finally he became a refugee. In 1689 he and his family fled and settled in Holland. He died in there in 1707.

Calvinists relied on local centres of Protestantism, such as Melle and Saint Maixent, to give support during these troubled times. In fact in one rural district, between Saint Maixent and Melle, seven of eight rural inhabitants were believed to be Protestant. By some calculations, at least 70 percent of Protestants in Poitou had come to live in Deux – Sèvres. Like others in their community, many Juchaults invoked coping mechanisms to ride out the storms of repression and made adjustments to their communal activities to avoid attention and to carry on their livelihoods. In present day Beaussais, Protestant families there recall past stories of their forbears, who kept their religious observances private in nearby woodlands, used areas on their farms to conduct family devotion services and invited others to come and participate.

Poitou first experienced more concerted anti-Calvinist campaigns in 1661. These involved special military decalvinising measures including the stationing of king's troops in Calvinist family homes to force conversion to the Catholic faith. For example, these measures occurred in the village of Foussais, where the king's troops, *dragonnades* or cavalry regiments, occupied Protestant homes and forced the occupants to abjure their protestant faith. Soldiers became one of the principal means to secure conversion.

Over the period, 1660-85, families experienced an acceleration of these measures, especially in the years 1681-5 under the direction of *Marillac*, the *Intendant* of Poitou. *Intendants*, under Louis XIV, were like viceroys, overseeing the judicial and financial affairs of their region, as well as enforcing the king's decrees. These measures included punitive taxes and intensifying and extending the billeting of king's soldiers in Protestant homes to force conversion. To illustrate, soldiers went to the village of Exoudun in 1666 to harass and convert local Calvinists. Soldiers assaulted, intimidated and abused householders, destroyed property and stole goods. They were also stationed at village exit points to prevent followers leaving their village. Soldiers became known as "booted missionaries" or the "dragonnades".

Marillac's activities generated protests and some international outcry and criticism. Louvois, concerned about the commercial damage in Poitou, urged Marillac to proceed warily and to lessen coercive actions. At times there was resistance against the soldiers. Villagers abused and harassed soldiers. On occasion it was claimed that small detachments of troops had to yield and leave. Public protest and alarm often greeted the troops as they moved into a village to arrest individuals and occupy houses. Anger with the soldiers was heightened when they took food as well as securing forage for their horses. Occupation put great strains on household economies.

Soldiers were present in Poitou well into the 18th century and, whether by their simple presence or by their interference, they generated fear, and it was not always apparent which families would suffer their forays, given the capriciousness of the military, the authorities and the Catholic clergy. The disruption generated by the troops had economic consequences including loss of agricultural production, losses of rents on farms, adverse effects on textile production and quality, as well as the decline of markets.

The archival records do not reveal whether any of the Juchault families directly experienced this harassment. Some, according to some abjuration lists, came forward to abjure their faith. By 1685, the soldiers had varying success in forcing abjurations and, depending on the locality, the percentage of Calvinists abjuring ranged between 25 to 75 percent. And they contributed, according to some estimates, to the emigration of nearly a quarter of the Reformed Poitou population, to follow their faith and seek their fortune in other lands. Marillac claimed that by 1681 around 36,000 people had converted and his successor, the *Intendant* Foucault, claimed that by 1686 almost all of the Protestants in Poitiers had converted.

Other accounts of the actions of *dragonnades* illustrate the lengths to which they went to enforce orders. In Niort in 1685, under the eyes of town officials and the mayor, it was reported that householders had property cast out on the street, internal furnishings smashed and personal property burnt. Women were verbally abused and threatened with execution. Men, even though openly pledging loyalty to the king but upholding their religion, were placed in dungeons and shackled in irons. Catholics were forbidden to give refuge to their Protestant neighbours. Any males transgressing their orders could be sent to the galleys.

In 1688 at a locality, Grand Ry, near Prailles, a congregation of Protestants, meeting in a meadow, was set upon by

Grand Ry Memorial Plaque

EN CE LIEU

SPECIALEMENT DE 1688 A 1706

SE REUNIRENT

DES ASSEMBLEES DU « DESERT »

L'UNE D'ELLES FUT SURPRISE

LE 22 FEVRIER 1688

IL Y EUT 200 PRISONNIERS

31 CONDAMNE AUX GALERS

ET 15 MARTYRS

GRAND-RY FUT RASE

EN SOUVENIR DE CEUX QUI

NOUS ONT PERMIS DE PRIER

DIEU EN PAIX AUJOURD'HUI

LA SOCIETE DE L'HISTOIRE

DU PROTESTANTISME FRANÇAIS – 1951

POITOU-SAINTONGE PROTESTANTS - 2002

dragonnades whilst they were at prayer. Several persons were killed, three were hanged and around 30 were sentenced to penal servitude. This incident gained wide notoriety and today Grand Ry has become an important memorial site for Protestants visiting Deux-Sèvres.

The authorities also set about destroying temples. The Juchaults must have been dismayed to see their local temple at La Mothe demolished in 1682. By 1685, psalm singing was banned in private homes, tithe collection was outlawed and mixed marriages were made illegal. Not surprisingly, across all Poitou a sizeable proportion of the Protestant population converted or emigrated and the decline was more severe in towns and less so in rural areas. These measures were well detailed by Jean Migault in his journal. Calvinists who converted were labelled as the *nouveaux convertis* or *nouveaux catholiques*.

Conversion success varied between towns. For example, in 1697 in St Maixent 3,400 converted from a potential of 18,000, whereas in Exoudun less than five percent initially converted. In Niort, depending on the locality, up to three out of four Protestants had converted by 1699. While it was generally believed that townsfolk converted more readily than their rural neighbours in localities such as in Deux-Sèvres, the records on abjuration numbers were unreliable and misleading. Conversion numbers were often overstated and abjuration lists were often shown to record the same name several times.

Many of the neighbours of Charles were converts in name only, whilst others complied with obligatory gestures to the church, such as attending mass and having priests conduct baptisms and marriages. There were variable records of numbers taking the Catholic communion. For many, who retained their Calvinist faith, these actions and conversions of their neighbours only reinforced their religious solidarity and intensified their desire to retain their faith. Worship became less open, and where it was communal, it occurred privately or secretly. It is not known how many of the Juchault families in Poitou maintained their faith over these troubled times.

At the close of the 17th century the actions of Louis XIV and his agents continued to intensify throughout Poitou and elsewhere, with the clear intention to finally remove Protestantism from Poitou. Actions included: prohibitions (e.g. emigration); banishments (e.g. Protestant ministers); conversions (e.g. baptisms). The effects of banishments in all of France can be seen in the loss of Protestant ministers. By 1685 it was estimated that 680 of the 870 ministers in France had gone into exile, while others converted or went into hiding. Especially harsh was the continuing prohibition on migration. For many Calvinists, avoiding conversion through emigration was the only way to secure their religious and economic futures.

Once pastors had been expelled, lay helpers took on pastoral work. The early performance record of pastors in their parish organisations, referred to as *consistoires,* had been subject to hyperbole and not all were successful in parish work. Lay helpers, termed *anciens,* assisted with pastoral care, including educating children, serving the poor, and taking strong stances against drunkenness, uncivil habits and disorder. The archive revealed that Charles had become a lay preacher. Accounts of pastoral activities were sometimes hazy, but many congregations received valuable assistance, leadership and service during the unfolding turbulence.

Charles had four options: he could remain Protestant, risking persecution; he could pretend to be Catholic feigning adherence; he could seek refuge, pursuing his faith in a new country; or he could formally convert, adhering to the prescriptions of the Catholic faith. Charles may have possibly abjured to ease his pathway to emigrate. It is not known what options the relatives of Charles pursued. Some present day French Juchaults believe that many of their forbears retained their Calvinist faith throughout, since there are only a few Juchault abjurations recorded. Some abjured because they wanted to keep their family together, maintain friendships and hold onto their possessions.

Observers noted that, amongst the Poitevins who formally converted, their levels of sincerity and their degree of adherence to the Catholic faith were variable. Some embraced the faith completely, others exhibited token adherence and sincerity, and others, having converted, returned to their Calvinist faith at the first opportune moment. Often their embrace of the faith was heavily influenced by other family members who did not abjure. Many surprisingly did not blame Louis XIV for the persecutions. They remained loyal to the king. Many believed he was advised badly by his officials and that the persecutions were the fault of his agents. To many he was the victim of bad counselling and misinformation.

Often it was the wealthier and more adventurous Huguenots also known locally as *parpaillots,* who fled abroad to avoid forced conversion, whilst those who remained retained their faith often using subterfuge. Normally they registered their faith with their *consistoire* which prepared lists of the faithful, *reformées,* and issued them *méreaux* – tokens or passes – a kind of ticket which authorised participation in the Calvinist assemblies. They attended clandestine church gatherings in secluded wooded areas, in the fields of family farms and in other remote locations such as in the Lambon valley near Mougon. The woods of middle Poitou became important for meetings. The woods lay within a triangle bounded by St Maixent, Mougon and Melle.

These assemblies were sometimes held at night in the shadow of the parasol pine, the tree which became a symbol of freedom. Many present-day Protestants plant the parasol pine on their properties as a symbol of remembrance and recognition of the sacrifices and troubles suffered in their localities. Some wealthy families often welcomed these meetings in their barns and houses.

These secret meetings were referred to as *assemblées du desert,* brought about the notion of the *culte du désert* or *wilderness* referring to the bible story of the years the Hebrews were homeless during the Exodus. The notion of *le Désert* was to become an identifying and rallying symbol for celebrating the Protestant faith in France right through to the present day. Some writers have referred to the period between 1680 and 1740, when these assemblies occurred, as a period of *Le Désert Héroïque.*

Fear and repression were ever present. In the absence of pastors, courageous lay protestant preachers, *prédicants,* whose activities were also under threat, endeavoured to keep the faith alive in their *consistoire.* Amongst the preachers, first noticed at Beaussais, was a woman known as *Robine la Bergère,* , who by 1697 had a reputation for impressive sermons. She was condemned by the Papists and adored by Calvinists. Preachers sustained strong cells of believers able to survive the inroads of the king's directives. Families, like the Juchaults, valued the presence of the cells to assist in assuring that a Calvinist presence was maintained in their localities. And according to the records, Charles had become a lay preacher before he departed for England.

As noted, observable Calvinist community activity dwindled as Calvinists converted, emigrated or withdrew to attend to their religious affairs privately. Many Calvinists had hoped by 1698, the centenary of the Edict of Nantes and in the wake of the Treaty of Rysdyk, that the king would revisit the provisions of the Revocation of 1685, and reverse many of the decrees. No relief was forthcoming and by December, anti-Calvinist measures were intensified, leading to more conversions and emigration. More nobles and bourgeoisie were converted but a strong core of Calvinists continued to uphold their faith.

It has been estimated that between the middle of the 17th century and the middle of the 18th century regional population loss was at its highest. In the period, 1680-1725 there were concentrations of refugee outflows from France, principally 1681-82, 1685-88, 1698-1701, 1709-15 and 1724. Many who fled included merchants, traders, artisans and professionals. In London, the two largest outflows, based on new arrivals joining the French congregations, were in the 1685-88 and 1698-1701 periods.

Observers noted that farmers and rural workers were less likely to leave since their wealth and social links were closely tied to the land and their villages. Their capital was immobile. A number Juchault families hold property today and their occupation can be traced back to the 18th century. Through their relative rural isolation, community solidarity and farming commitments, the pressure to leave was lessened and as well, gave them a capacity to passively resist the actions of authorities. In some cases, the isolation of rural households became a barrier to authorities trying to enforce the orders of the crown. Nevertheless many took the risky option to leave, prepared to disregard royal decrees outlawing emigration and to face the consequences of being arrested by the authorities.

Apart from Charles and Louis, all the other Juchaults appear to have remained in Poitou and, like their neighbours who remained, they had to survive through mutual assistance and collective endurance. Many played a double game, conforming to requirements of the monarch state, but all the while resisting directives and sustaining Protestant beliefs and traditions. Outward conformity and inner faithfulness became the common mode of surviving. Many women, whose husbands had abjured to preserve family position and wealth, remained Protestant and discreetly preserved the faith and its practices in their families. These women became primary conveyors of religious traditions, both within households and at religious assemblies.

All through these times, there were many reports of individuals and small groups taking overt action to profane the Catholic Church and its rituals. They disrupted services and displayed irreverence and mocked the sacred undertakings. Some disrupted services by chanting and speaking out loudly during a priest's formal address. These outbreaks of irreverence did indicate a spirit of resistance as well as contempt for the formalities of the Catholic service.

Although the communities could be considered as being divided along religious lines, Poitou Calvinists, in the main, had cordial relations with Catholic neighbours, and tensions generally only arose with authorities. They maintained a simple form of piousness throughout and upheld a passive or muted form of resistance. They did not take up arms to resist nor did they appear to adopt a form of religious exuberance, a form of devotion which was known then as "prophesy" as practised in the region of Languedoc. This region conducted an active resistance where guerrilla warfare was waged by armed Calvinists (*Camisards*) who frustrated the monarch's measures and the conversion efforts of authorities. The *Camisards* operated over the 1702-15 period and their efforts became scattered after severe fighting in 1704. The knowledge that Protestants in other parts of France were resisting must have given comfort to Poitou Protestants resolved to uphold their religion.

Those disregarding the law and authorities, suffered badly when arrested. In both regions men were generally punished with penal servitude in French navy galleys, women were imprisoned in catholic hospitals and nunneries and children were placed in convents. Some faced execution. The threat of convents often led to young women to marry to avoid incarceration. And for many families this threat weakened their Calvinist resolve and they converted to keep families together.

In Poitou religious prisoners grew from 200 odd in 1690 to around 800 by 1700. One estimate had around 170 men from Poitou sent to the galleys. No Juchault appeared in records from the galleys and convents. Over the period 1680-1740, Poitou witnessed 14 death sentences and around 750 sent to the galleys or imprisoned.

Some priests in Poitou took uncompromising positions towards their Protestant communities and were openly hostile and condemning. They ridiculed Calvinism and claimed that it was not a real religion and undeserving of recognition. In their eyes it was a *religion prétendue réformée*. Some however were less diligent, either by intent or incompetence, and did not pursue the directions of their bishops and authorities, allowing both their local Calvinists and new converts to pursue their lives without interference or public criticism.

There were clergy, however, who showed compassion for the plight and tragedy of their Calvinist neighbours and gave them both pastoral service and assistance, as well as pleading to their superiors for more tolerance and acceptance of Calvinism.

The worst case of Catholic zealousness was the disentombment of Protestants, followed by a formal trial of the dead and dragging the "guilty" bodies through the village and the dumping them in a ditch at the end of a village.

It was only adherents of the Catholic faith who could act as public officials and hold certain professional positions, including medicine and law. Charles' relatives, like other Protestants, carried on their rural pursuits. Village cohesion and strength often stymied any directive to curtail their work. Restrictions on normal commercial transactions were applied to both the newly converted and the unconverted. Despite these restrictions local social conditions allowed many Protestants to continue to carry out their jobs because strong community ties and respect meant that restrictions were largely ignored or were unenforceable.

Catholic priests acted as agents in administering many of the orders issued by authorities. Some priests denounced the Protestants in their parishes and reported the unfaithful to authorities. However, the enforcement actions of priests and authorities varied in intensity across parishes and time periods. In some localities, as a result of the religious wars, the Catholic Church had lost leverage and presence and therefore it was unable to fulfil its obligations. On legal actions some judges, for example, took tolerant and benevolent stances often dismissing actions against Protestants because allegations were unfounded or simply unjust.

In the Poitou communities, there was a large percentage of Calvinists employed as farmers, ploughmen, farm workers and craftsmen. Mostly they remained in their locality. Some, however, were also on the move to settle in districts and villages where Protestantism had a stronger following.

For example, Prailles eventually had 90 percent of its population Protestant. Some villages, Exoudun and La Mothe, experienced little loss in their Protestant congregations. La Mothe, between 1618 and 1685, maintained a membership around 350-360. Because temples had been destroyed and pastors had returned to Switzerland or had fled elsewhere abroad, the communities had to wait until 1720 before pastors returned to lead assemblies, often using aliases to escape attention. More were to return by the mid 18th century as restrictions and prohibitions were eased or not pursued.

The larger towns of Niort and St Maixent both retained a core Protestant group able to keep their religion alive. Authorities complained however that by 1698 the rural areas were still "infested" with Calvinist heretics. Many, who appeared to abjure and adhere to Catholic rituals, nevertheless undertook the challenging tasks of having baptisms, marriages and funerals carried out in accordance with Calvinist practice. Burials took place in private gardens or in a corner of a private field. Many families also buried their dead on their farm properties, since it was forbidden for Protestants to bury their dead in parish graveyards, which were Catholic controlled. These family burial sites, including those of a number of Juchault families, continue to be maintained throughout present-day Poitou.

Apart from the decrease in the Protestant population in Poitou, around 50 percent between 1670 and 1720, Charles could observe the changing composition of his neighbours following the surge of conversions, the relocation of families and the increasing emigration flows. Local Protestant nobles had converted as well as many of the middle class. Rural and artisan workers became the core of Calvinism in parts of Deux-Sèvres, where farming continued to sustain the wealth of the community.

Throughout these unsettling times good relations between many Calvinist and Catholic families were maintained benefiting agricultural production and trade. Catholics, including the newly converted, generally had, as noted, amicable relations with their Protestant neighbours and rarely informed authorities about Protestant gatherings. Many of the newly converted were poor converts, failing to attend mass and remained unruly in the Church's eyes. There were reports that Catholics were troubled by the decrees and did not denounce assemblies. Some even attended assemblies out of curiosity or at the invitation of predicants. Priests were known not to condemn members of their flock attending assemblies. A group of Catholics in the village of Benet left and refused to attend the hanging of a local Calvinist. Nevertheless a number of Catholics and "turncoat" Protestants were prepared to spy and inform authorities of Calvinists in their midst.

Mixed marriages did occur and often raised the ire of priests who referred to these marriages as a "grand scandale". One observer noted that the boundary between the two faiths was porous. And these conditions may have moderated the urge to move away. Perhaps this partly explains why so many Juchaults remained in Poitou.

Movements between faiths, ineffective social barriers and weak confessional identity kept social interactions relatively healthy. As a result it was not surprising that allegiance to Calvinism in many communities never became strident. It possibly hardened in some areas where the measures of Louis XIV were severe. Fanatical Catholics were reported to be quite hostile to their Catholic brethren who exhibited tolerance and respect for Protestants. Still it was noteworthy that ordinary Catholic citizens in parts of Poitou appeared to see Calvinism as unthreatening and did not consider its followers as fanatics. It was noted in some records that the ties of friendship remained strong and that confessional co-existence was the norm throughout parts of Poitou.

It appears then that, in Poitou, there were no hermetically sealed communities of belief and customs and, between faiths, the interpenetration of many religious and cultural practices occurred. For example, many Protestant families, perhaps in respect of Catholic sensibilities, observed the restrictions (such as marriage) surrounding the periods of Lent and Advent. As well, the superstitious belief in the unluckiness of May marriages (*Creux de Mai*) was shared by both faiths, especially in the 17th century. For the most part, it appears that, whilst suppressive measures hit many Calvinists hard, there was a level of amiable coexistence and common adherence to local customs amongst the two faiths.

Nevertheless conditions – social, economic, political and religious – would have presented Charles with an accumulating impression that prospects were unlikely to change and a brighter future lay elsewhere. It is hard to judge which of the push or pull factors loomed hard in his mind. It is not possible to determine whether Huguenot victimhood was telling and that he left France for the sake of his religion. Nor is it possible to ascertain whether misfortune or poor economic conditions were also factors. There are no records to guide on this matter. He probably saw light in the emigrant tunnel and the local religious and economic upheavals had little prospect of diminishing in the future. He opted for the risky and costly option to emigrate. He left to what promised to be a better world.

Sections of the Protestant community of Poitou revealed a core of stubbornness and endurance. They managed to frustrate the monarch and uphold religious pluralism. The efforts of the monarch and his agents were never able to claim a victory. Whilst many Protestants converted or fled, a core of believers held firm and did not yield. The conversions were often a "façade" and "new" Catholics maintained normal relationships. A surprising number withstood the punitive measures. They gave Poitou a special place in Calvinist history. They demonstrated that groups with strong principles based on faith or community can prevail. Freedom of conscience and association were important rights to uphold.

Charles, in leaving Poitou may have reflected on this character of his community. Not long after he had departed, a wave of religious fervour rose amongst Poitou Calvinists, who assembled in the location of demolished temples, such as La Mothe and Melle, only to face again in 1718 renewed bouts of repression by the agents of the new king, Louis XV. He may have suspected that, despite the rhetoric of success trumpeted by the French ecclesiastical and the civil authorities, the total extirpation of Poitou Protestants was never likely to succeed.

CHAPTER 4
Charles-Refugee and London

Committed Protestant families and reluctant new converts were in a classic bind of whether to stay or leave France. Reports from emigrants in England continued to flow back, painting a picture of favourable conditions for religious freedom, economic opportunity and good prospects for building a new life. The hazards, costs and dangers of leaving France were widely known. Charles would have heard about the well-known routes for fleeing the country, for example, whether to go to the south west through La Rochelle and head for North America, England or Ireland or to go north west perhaps through Normandy and then to England or elsewhere. In London, Poitevins found support in the French churches, such as La Patente and La Pénitence. The first French church there was established in 1550 in a chapel of the hospital in Threadneedle Street. In Ireland, they often made their way to Antrim. Others sought passage through Normandy to Holland and east towards Germany and Switzerland.

Charles having sensed that his prospects in rural Poitou were uncertain, may have received family blessing to head for England and London where other Poitevins had established a foothold. He and his family may have received accounts of life and conditions in London from returning Poitevins or from accounts received in their community.

In the England of King James II, prospects for Protestants had improved by 1687, when a Toleration Act was passed giving freedom of worship to Catholics, Protestants and other dissenters. Conditions for Protestants improved further following the Glorious Revolution of 1688, when the Dutch Protestant King William III, Prince of Orange, invaded England and succeeded James II. His invasion was the only successful invasion of England since 1066. His intention was to stop England falling under the influence of Louis XIV. London, then with a population of half a million people, and with growing commerce and emerging industry, experienced an influx of immigrants, both skilled and unskilled.

Whilst his rural community were partly shielded from the excesses of the authorities, Charles would have received stories about the actions of Foucault, the king's intendant, who carried out repressive measures with great zeal over the 1685-9 period. Foucault had previous experience of applying decalvinising measures in Béarn. In the early years of the 1700s Charles saw the effects of the taxes set by the king to sustain his war with England as well as the long war of Spanish succession (1701-1713), which was claimed to be 'the first world war' since it was fought in Germany, the Netherlands, Italy, Spain and their colonies. He would have also felt the renewed efforts by intendants to punish Protestants.

In 1709 the disastrous effects of the coldest European winter for 500 years were taking hold. His community, like the rest of France, saw crops fail, animals die, soils and vegetation freeze. There were three months of deadly cold which ushered in a year of famine, mass migration, disease, endemic crime and high food prices. Starvation and distress were evident and reports had ordinary people subsisting on a diet of bark, berries and beet. Over 600,000 people perished in France. The country was also facing a financial crisis as wealth was destroyed, debts were unpaid, taxes uncollected and where the strain of wars had hit the king's treasury hard. The state's finances were in grave disarray. In many regions open and bloody revolts were occurring such as in Languedoc (1703-9) and had to be put down by the military.

This disaster together with a mixture of religious, economic and social factors possibly drove Charles to leave. It is not possible to discern what information he possessed about his destination, his travel route, and his chances of employment. His decision to leave home was unlikely to have been taken in a fit of religious enthusiasm, as one observer has described the rush to emigrate. He no doubt saw that that the benefits of migration outweighed the costs and risks involved. He and Louis were to become the first Juchaults to step on English soil and to enter an immigrant life.

Charles Juchault, a young man, accompanied by a younger relative, Louis, most probably moved west to seek a route to England. He most likely had a handful of farming or craft skills, a fragment of literacy and no English. His language, *Poitevin*, was one of the many dialects in the group of dialects based on the then language of northern France – *langues d'oil*. It is not known whether he had converted to Catholicism and changed the spelling of his name to avoid difficulties. His big challenge was to translate from a rural to an alien urban setting. The challenge may have been understood, because communication links with London were strong with Poitou. Local families had fetched up in London and with their help and from other Huguenots, he could anticipate some assistance with the settlement transition. He did not share the experiences of most refugees today, where support and reception would be uncertain or unavailable.

As he passed through his district making his way to England, he would have had some regrets in leaving an area where the lifeblood and opportunity of agriculture were apparent. If he traversed the areas familiar to his extended family, he would have passed through wheat growing areas and, depending on topography, he would have observed a variety of animal and other crop production. The barley, rye, oats, the groves of walnuts and chestnuts, the presence of cattle, horses, mules, and sheep all would have reminded him of his district's diverse agriculture. He would be quite aware that there was competition for land use between cereal cropping and pastures for fodder and hay making.

The sometimes unreliable agricultural bounty produced in his region, together with rural garden produce, must have weighed heavily on his decision to leave, since the most humble of his neighbours had access to basic foods and fuels to provide a bearable life. This bounty was often set back by adverse climate conditions, such as the terrible winter of 1709. Then local people faced famine and had to resort to eating meals of vetch to survive. Normally his community was self-sustaining and productive and had shown its recovery capacity when it was able to emerge from the earlier famine of 1693.

Yet these favourable memories of agricultural life would have been blighted by the disruption of life brought about by the actions of Louis XIV and their effects on the society, economy, demography and structure of his community. He would have observed that the economy was being run down and the moral fabric weakened. Those principal towns of Poitou, famous for their manufactures, saw their artisans and craftsmen emigrate. Also compounding the problem was emigration to village centres from the countryside where some pastures and fields were abandoned. In the area between Niort and La Mothe over one fifth of its inhabitants had moved away. Skills and wealth had shifted elsewhere. Key workers and traders had also decamped. He no doubt would have seen this decline and depopulation as a high price to pay, so that the king could have one religion for France.

He may have passed through Beaussais, Mougon, or St Maixent on his journey and reflected on how these villages, including La Mothe, brought communities together for festivals, fairs and market days. Farm produce markets and fairs were critical to improving the economic and social conditions of the region and there was rivalry between the markets such as Melle and St Maixent. But village conditions may have also promoted reasons to emigrate. The visible signs of repression of his religion were apparent with destroyed temples and the loss of other symbols of Calvinist life. People gathered at markets, which were important points for new information about comparative developments and prospects locally and abroad. And the presence and actions of the king's soldiers may have confirmed in his mind that the repression, even though it was haphazardly applied, was always likely.

Today, the department from where Charles came, retains it rural and agricultural character. Travellers and visitors are delivering economic benefits to the region through tourism and recreation, which are generating wealth alongside agriculture. Various sub-regions, Mellois, Niortais, Marais Poitevin, Thouarsais and Bressurais attract visitors. Fields of corn, canola, sunflowers and wheat are evident in the undulating landscape, crisscrossed by streams and dotted with woodlands. Intensive and extensive farming of animals are apparent. Cattle, sheep, geese, chickens and goats dot the landscape. Nut groves are present and modern roads link the villages and major towns. Watermills have become tourist sites and market days generate local and visitor trade.

The spread of small villages, while today linked by sealed roads, confirms the view that their disbursement and relatively isolated situations gave these rural and farm communities some protection from interfering authorities and afforded a privacy not enjoyed in the towns. And the ever present parasol pines across the rural landscape serve as a reminder of Huguenot heritage, including historical localities and burial sites. Many farmers continue to plant the pine as a way of acknowledging its symbolic importance.

Villages like La Mothe, Exoudun and St Maixent, retain their civic importance, but many old dwellings there are in need of restoration. They require extensive masonry and tile work to bring them back to a habitable condition. Local traders and shops have lost their trade to the super centres encircling village outskirts while cafés, bars and the ubiquitous bakery, together with market days in town squares, keep some vibrancy in their centres.

Temples have been rebuilt but they have small congregations. Some do not offer weekly services. They are served by visiting pastors, many of whom are Lutheran trained. Protestant communities have declined as the exodus from rural life continues and the indifference to religion has grown. The Protestant flame has been kept alive by Protestant associations, researchers and archives. Through commercial museums and tourist sites, the significance of Calvinist heritage for national and international visitors also is kept alive.

Charles must have shared the fear of others as he took to the road to find a ship to England. Fear was real, as the king prohibited migration in 1699 and increased actions to imprison those caught leaving France and to confiscate their property. Charles' options were to sail from La Rochelle or from one of the Channel ports in Brittany or Normandy. It is not known which port he chose at the time, but it is likely he followed a traditional route, popular with Poitevins, travelling west and northwards, perhaps in a group with a guide, through villages where a number of residents provided shelter and security.

Guides would receive payment for their work. Payment was often determined through negotiation and bargaining. Guides knew that their refugees would be generally accepted by their country of destination. This contrasts with present day people smugglers where acceptance is problematical. Fear of capture was ever present. Those captured were given severe galley or prison sentences and guides were often executed. In 1715, a guide, Pierre Michaut, was executed in the main square of La Mothe. It is unlikely that Charles would have departed through La Rochelle given that arrests of Poitevins there had been on the increase.

A probable route was to head towards Granville via Parthenay, Angers and Laval or via Nantes and Vitré. At Granville he could go to England via Jersey or he could head further north to one of the ports of Normandy and gain passage there. He would have needed funds to pay for safe guidance, accommodation and for a boat passage to England. Travelling would have been hazardous and the areas through which he would have passed had few Protestants to assist his progress. Many *Poitevins* had been captured on their way north and suffered severely. Vigilance and resourcefulness would have been displayed by those on their exile passage. He may have arrived at Dover, following a voyage of several days and made his way to London through Kent and, at Gravesend, he could have taken a boat up the River Thames.

What were the challenges facing Charles? We can only conjecture through the accounts of others. He came from a rural setting. It is highly unlikely that he had a trade or profession and his resources would likely have been limited. There were no entries of his name in church records of early 18th century London recording his arrival. We can conjecture also that he may have been infused with some of the French Protestant ethos to seek gainful employment and a vocation. It is likely that he had a small amount of money. Most of his funds would have been used to finance his journey and passage to London.

He probably joined a number of refugees from Poitou, seeking links with settled Poitevins in London. His options were to find cheap housing in the west around Soho or in the east around Spitalfields. One estimate had Poitevins making up 35 percent of the 20,000 or more refugees settling in London between 1670 and 1710. And in London, the French presence may have been of comfort to him. By 1700 there were over 20 Huguenot churches in London, both in the West End and in and around the eastern end. It was reported that by 1711 the parish of St Anne's in Soho had 40 percent of its population French.

Records of his arrival date in London were not found. There is no record of him presenting a *témoinage* certificate which was used to prove a person's Calvinist faith. They were not issued by *consistoires* after1685. If he had converted, there is no record of him renouncing his Catholicism, which many of his fellow refugees managed to do shortly after their arrival. This was a means to gain acceptance and integration into the community. Others, to affirm their Calvinism, made a *reconnaissance* to a congregation, outlining their life and faith before, during and after their passage of exile. His relative, Louis, is recorded as making his *reconnaissance* in 1716.

The fact that most of his male direct descendants took on unskilled and low-skilled work such as paviors (*paveurs*) is perhaps an indication that he had little wealth to provide basic education. While there is no direct evidence that he had converted to Catholicism, he most probably had considered conversion to make his life easier and perhaps to secure arrangements for leaving France.

He arrived in his new country which had undergone major political change. The Act of Union of 1707 created the United Kingdom of Great Britain and the unification of the British monarchy. Apart from the cohesive benefits of the ascendancy of the crown, Britain also was on the cusp of being a colonial power, advanced by the Treaty of Utrecht of 1713 and the growing supremacy of British naval power.

In prospering Georgian London he would have noted that other refugees were fitting into the strengthening economy and adapting to demands from emerging technologies and a growing international commerce. He would have observed strengthening religious pluralism, unlike in France where the quest for mono-religion continued unabated. At this time, he would have found sympathy amongst many of his fellow Londoners, who appreciated that they were brethren in religion, deserving of compassion and understanding. As well, he would have shared with them a hatred of the much reviled Louis XIV and his persecution of Huguenots.

Nevertheless it was reported that life was not all smooth sailing, since there was insularity and distrust amongst some Londoners towards the French refugees. Resentment and fear were observed as locals saw their jobs and community charities threatened. Xenophobia was clearly present. Many refugees, especially those who had skills or wealth behind them, were able to shield themselves by having strong households and developing successful commercial connections. Others, who were poor and unskilled, may have felt this resentment more. They were able to seek charitable and community support which may have cushioned any community antagonism. Work and relief was provided to ease their transition and somewhat lessening the impact of any local hostility.

Charles headed for the area of St Giles in the Field, where housing and food were cheaper and casual work prospects existed. He may have found the sights and smells there displeasing in contrast to his former rural setting. The area attracted poor immigrants, especially in the area north of St Giles High Street as far as Great Russell Street. Perhaps when Charles reached there, it had not deteriorated to the state which Dickens, a century later, described as "a compound of sickening smells containing heaps of filth and tumbling houses with animate and inanimate vile contents slimily overflowing into the black road". The Irish had come to the area in 1625, followed by Armenians and Greeks in 1640 and then later in the century the French refugees. By 1710 there was large Huguenot population living in and around St Giles.

Charles found employment there as a baker, and his lodgings may have presented abysmal living conditions. St Giles, with its squalid housing, disorder, and insecurity gained a notorious reputation. Many writers of both 18th and 19th centuries considered the area as the epitome of slum living, exacerbated by the presence of thieves, vagrants and prostitutes. Serious social and health problems arose from the wide-spread consumption of gin, the appalling sanitation and the high level of crime.

His relative, Louis, headed for Spitalfields. By 1720, this area had a population of around 21,000 housed in 2200 dwellings occupied by artificers, weavers, labourers and the unemployed. Most struggled to support their families. Many refugees found work in the burgeoning East End silk weaving industry. During the latter part of the 17th century, the arrival of weavers from France had boosted the industry by bringing new silk technologies including lustrings and alamodes. By 1750 around Spital Square, there were 500 master weavers and 15,000 looms at work. Over 50,000 Londoners were dependant on this trade. The observation – "weavers raised their families to be weavers" – was a common saying.

The whole silk weaving industry had become synonymous with the Spitalfields locality, a hamlet of Stepney within the parish of Christchurch. The industry and weavers suffered badly from trade cycles, competition and fashion changes, as well as the wage depression from cheaper labour sources which included women, children and immigrants from Ireland. During depressed times, workers took to protest and rioting, especially as cheaper labour displaced local workers. Starvation and misery were often felt by the industry workers. The area also had merchants and trades such as engraving and watchmaking.

For poorer arrivals like Charles, most work was generated through London being a seaport, as well as a manufacturing and craftwork hub and a centre for services and goods required by a growing middle-class. London was becoming a major centre of population and a great emporium. It contained a full spectrum of street merchants, artisans, craftsmen, tradesmen and labourers. Intensive and regular manual work, on civic improvement projects for water, roads and sanitation, had yet to emerge as a major source of employment for the unskilled. It was not to gain significance until the 1760s when extensive paving, lighting and sanitation works commenced.

Charles would find nearby Huguenot churches offering comfort to refugees. There were also French friendly societies, some of which had regional linkages, providing relief to the poor and sick. Suffering from the challenges, perils and anxieties accompanying his passage and the depletion of funds, he may have joined others seeking assistance to ease the settlement pathway. As with many fellow refugees, he had to adapt to secure a living. Whether his upbringing and character and or Poitevin networks assisted him in gaining a foothold in London is not clear.

Charles married Elizabeth Sibley from Soho in 1725 at Fleet Prison. Charles only used one Christian name, Charles, for marriage registration and the record is the first time a change is noted in spelling of his surname. He now was registered as Juchau. He had a second Christian name Lewis (Louis). At the time, it was common to use one or both and sometime to reverse their order. He appeared in various records as Charles, Lewis, Lewis Charles, or Charles Lewis. Fleet prison served as a debtors' prison and held many disgraced clergymen, many in debt, who conducted less expensive services to earn income. It was a popular option for the poor unable to marry in an Anglican church or who wished to keep their marriage private.

Charles and Elizabeth had nine children, the first being born in 1729 and the last in 1748 and all were raised in St Giles. Five of the children did not survive early childhood. His surviving four children were Thomas (1739-1806), Daniel (1735-1767), Lewis (1741-1787) and Philip (1748-1765). Charles died in 1756.

As history has shown he would have observed that the vestiges of French background were quickly lost by his fellow refugees, who quickly integrated and appeared not to be fazed by urban London's idiosyncrasies. The second generation mostly married outside the French community and this hastened assimilation and identity loss. His remaining offspring married Londoners and were quick to adopt London habits, customs, argot and mostly used common English Christian names for their children. Most settled in the Spitalfields, Shoreditch and Bethnal Green localities. Most of his descendants became members of the Anglican Church. Charles left them no written memoirs recounting his past. No account was passed down explaining why he left Poitou and his experiences of departing and arriving.

It was apparent that Charles and his immediate descendants had been caught up in the mimetic urge to assimilate and to adopt customs of their host neighbourhood. Charles' circumstances meant that he was not in a position to preserve his Huguenot identity which many Huguenot leaders championed. It would appear he did not join those refugees who defined themselves as innocent victims, suffering from sustained persecution and fanaticism.

Refugee ministers and other community leaders, who often publicised the plight and suffering of Huguenot refugees, had hoped that enduring Huguenot enclaves would form and prosper, retaining both language and liturgy. It was argued that maintaining a separate identity would ease the return to France once conditions permitted. However the poor like Charles could not countenance such an outcome, given the economic and social order of his new community as well as the imperatives of life flowing from a dynamic and cosmopolitan London. While it might have appeared to Charles that strong and enduring French bastions could be seen as desirable, nevertheless the practicalities and challenges of life in London ruled that they were never a prospect.

His poor neighbourhood, dominated by Irish migrants, somehow absorbed the inflow of French refugees. It had congested housing where each house, often in a ramshackle state, was multi-occupied and heavily overcrowded. Poor and cramped housing conditions were exacerbated by large families. Health standards were inhibited by rudimentary sanitation. Often families had 8 to 12 children to support and faced high rates of infant mortality. The better-off enjoyed furnished rooms, whilst others rented rooms in substandard lodgings.

His relative, Louis Juchault, married Anne Giraud in 1718 and they had five children. Louis made his *reconnaissance* in 1716 and witnessed many Protestant baptisms. He died in 1725.The records had his name spelt Juchau as well as a number of misspellings. Anne Giraud remarried in1728, and passed away in1739. It is not clear whether the wives of Charles and Louis had come from France around the time of their husbands or had known them previously. They had French names and may have come from Poitou where their family names were present in the area.

Louis settled in Spitalfields, formerly open ground and fields. It enjoyed some industry, especially weaving and cloth-finishing. It remained locked in poverty, despite a rise in prosperity and living standards, which London was enjoying at this time. The silk-weaving industry, originally established in Whitechapel and Shoreditch, had spread to Stepney and Spitalfields and from there to spread to local-ities like Bethnal Green. The industry led to the growth of housing, warehouses and workshops. Observers noted that despite the prospect of poverty, there was nevertheless a positive atmosphere amongst many Huguenots whose skills, social vigour, individual endeavour and creativity gave the area some distinction.

Most of Louis' and Charles' descendants settled in the areas of Spitalfields and Shoreditch. They experienced hard conditions, joining "struggle street" and coping with large families, changing industry and tough employment conditions. Many families were forced to move eastwards to cheaper housing in Bethnal Green, which previously had been a rural area with many dairy farms. It quickly became a hamlet of retreat, filled with inferior housing and attracting the poor and those facing continuing unemployment and hardship.

It is hard to visualise how Charles dealt with his encounters in London. Accounts of French refugees are for the most part from those with wealth and connections. Their stories, while revealing the challenges of flight, often reported their movement, as what one observer noted, into enclaves of kin and former neighbours, conserving for a period their social networks, language, customs and religion. In his neighbourhood, Charles would have encountered the full spectrum of poverty, destitution and drudgery as well as drunkenness and violence. Some arrivals felt alienated and were not prepared to stay and either returned to France or moved elsewhere.

Charles never returned. He weathered the difficulties and found ways to exist in his new milieu. His marriage and children must have given him both pleasure and a sense of belonging. A generation of Juchaus was now to make England home. We do not know whether he ever contemplated returning to France or journeying to the Huguenot settlements in the New World. Nor do we know whether his family in Poitou ever received news from this emerging branch in England.

It is also impossible to construct the life of Charles without diaries, letters and accounts. His habits, housing and social milieu in both countries can be speculated about, but his personal journeys and his views remain hidden. In London, which was in the transition from medieval conditions, he must have been struck by the adverse and compact conditions of urban life of the poor, especially housing, health, sanitation, pollution and mortality rates.

Fresh food was obtained from market stalls as well as from porters and carriers, who did the rounds selling perishable food. Deliveries could be secured for coal, milk and water. The diet of meat and root vegetables was evident and the presence of ale and gin houses and breweries may have struck a novel note. The widespread presence of cheap and intoxicating liquor, which was sold indiscriminately, was evident. It was observed that liquor was a popular option to drinking polluted water. The human consequences of what was termed an "orgy of spirit drinking" left a mark on neighbourhoods. Sanitation was a constant problem because of inadequate housing arrangements and poor public health standards. Sewerage and refuse were most often left uncollected, and filthy conditions were experienced around houses and in the streets. Most human and industrial waste was dumped or washed down into the Thames. The stench was ever present. Water was not always clean and no water purification existed.

As a newcomer with limited means he would share the impressions and experiences of others making a new life in London, now a restless sea of humanity. He would have feelings of bewilderment, loneliness and some alienation. He would encounter offensive odours, foul air, fogs, noise and the sounds of the movements of carts, animals, markets and the throngs of people. He would observe a fascinating range of accents, dress styles, customs, religious practices and ethnicities. He may have been shocked by large numbers of beggars, vagrants and deserted children roaming the streets and alleys. In his community, he would have observed the impact of irregularity of work and low wages. He would have missed the stabilities and relationships of village life and been challenged by the urban chaos around his new home.

His dislocation and apprehension perhaps would have been offset by the closeness of his neighbourhood which, sometimes unruly and turbulent, offered a sense of belonging and involvement in local events. Neighbours shared feast days, street life offered high social interaction and neighbours would come forward to assist families with births, deaths and marriages and help alleviate the stresses of unemployment and poverty. The widowed, the orphaned and the destitute often found support. The pall of high infant mortality, which he also experienced, and the high incidence of deaths from outbreaks of diseases also would have been confronting.

His choice to live and raise a family in St Giles would suggest that he had exhausted most of his funds leaving France. St Giles, as noted, had a reputation of being squalid with many overcrowded tenements and hovels often in a labyrinth of passageways, blind alleys, lanes and courts. Suffering and crime generated an unsavoury environment. Housing there was known as rookeries which today are referred to as slums. Surroundings, often degraded and filthy, were congested by the density of families occupying these tenements, as well as the presence of overcrowded lodging houses. The locality was known to be pestilential. Whole families lived one in room and a tenement might have the landlord plus four or five many families crammed in. Unsurprisingly, unhygienic conditions and ill health became the norm. Furnishings and bedding were minimal and whole families were known to share one bed.

He would have noted that many jobs, outside artisan work, focused on service, journeymen work and, where feasible, apprenticeships. Work was cyclical and irregular. Many sought casual work in construction, markets, the docks and transport. And he would have noted too that crime of all varieties was present, particularly crime against property, including house robbery, pick-pocketing, and shop lifting. Theft and drunkenness plighted his neighbour-hood. The road to survival entailed securing affordable rents, maintaining a basic diet, gaining access to work, and where possible, gaining for members of the family some form of income in whatever jobs were available.

Charles would have encountered or heard reports of public riots, protests and disturbances. For example, weavers rioted over the imports of foreign goods, such as calicos, and these riots required the intervention of troops to prevent more disruption. No doubt he would have been aware of these events and his views about them as a newcomer would have been interesting.

If Charles were to visit his neighbourhood today, he would see it undergoing major transformation. St Giles is in the heart of London's West End where theatres, restaurants, apartments, office complexes and mixed retail and commercial activities, all vie for business. Available property sites command high prices, while heritage and other authorities try to preserve elements of the area's former life. He would recognise one or two streets and he may have understood the assimilation struggles of its current Asian business immigrant communities, who have successfully gained a foothold in many parts. In a sense, a parallel can be drawn by these communities and Huguenots. They both embraced

London through enterprise and industriousness. They adjusted to conditions by mimetic behaviour and applying their communal energies to further the prospect of their communities.

In the social vortex of Georgian London, where many visitors and inhabitants found pleasure and excitement and where wealth was being amassed, Charles remained on the margin. He would have observed the social and economic cues flowing in a city where the beacons of opportunity and freedom remained strong but mostly elusive. The experience of poverty was widely felt. He found freedom but did not find his way on the road to fortune. It is not known how much he relayed to his children about life in Poitou, his flight to England and the experiences of hardship and martyrdom.

By the time of his death in1756, Charles may have begun to see changes in train to make London a better place to live for the poor, where reforms on health, public hygiene, public order and education, together with falling death rates and better policing were destined to have positive effects. Visible improvements to drainage, sanitation, street lighting and paving were underway and medical services, through hospitals infirmaries and dispensaries, were improving.

His descendants, given their 19th century London addresses and occupations, their large families, and the public records of their family circumstances, clearly continued to struggle and poverty always threatened.

His enterprise to leave France and take up the challenge of a London life was a remarkable achievement. His success in establishing and providing for a family most probably gave him his most valuable reward for venturing abroad. His descendants made their way, but in a London which continued to grow and prosper, they remained part of its struggling working class. Some did leave London and found their way to USA and Australia, finding themselves, like

Charles, in new lands where they had to carve out new lives and seek their fortune.

Many writers have argued that most Huguenot refugees, despite the conditions promoting their emigration, had more power and choice in their search for a place of settlement compared to modern day refugees. In some respects they shaped some of the conditions under which they settled and, in many new homelands, they had sympathy and support from their host communities and were regarded as desirable immigrants. Others argued that a considerable number of Huguenots were not passive victims and were able to control many aspects of the conditions of their migration. Charles, on the basis of his circumstances and of his origins, livelihood and housing, did not enjoy the level of power and support that many of his fellow refugees enjoyed. It is likely that the degree of choice in his place of settlement was more restricted than those with wealth, professional skills, and established trade connections. They were able to enjoy a more comfortable settlement transition.

Map London Growth 1690-1785

Chapter 5
James in England

Born at Batemans Row, Shoreditch, in June 1814, James was the second child of James Juchau and Sarah Milton, who married in1809. He was baptised as an Anglican at St. Leonards Church, Shoreditch in September 1814.

His father James was born in 1769. His grandfather, Thomas, was born in1739. His great grandfather was Charles, the French refugee, whose life in London has been described. Apart from Charles they were all paviors, eking out a marginal existence and supporting large families in the East End of London where social distress, poverty and human misery were experienced.

James was the second of nine siblings. He had four brothers and four sisters, and when he died in 1897, he had outlived them all but one. They all had little or no education and the boys were expected to find jobs to support the family.

His father James, and his mother Sarah, both died in 1852, and most of their siblings and their relatives lived in the Shoreditch, Bethnal Green ad Hackney districts. Their last child, John, was born in 1832. Their nine children put a strain on household life. Income, from whatever source, would have been welcome. James Senior had himself grown up in a family of 11 children and would have experienced hardship and struggle.

In common with most of their neighbourhood, the family had little wealth and owned no property. London, whilst giving opportunity to many, meant poverty to most. Their poorly housed neighbourhood had seen the overspill of workers, especially poor weavers, and their district, Bethnal Green, once a rural and market garden area, saw its population grow from 15,000 in 1750 to 85,000 by 1850.

James' grandfather Thomas, a pavior who died in 1806, sought other means of income to support his family by taking up prize fighting. Known as 'Juchau the Swiss' he fought more than a hundred bouts and was crowned English Champion in 1765. A property was bought in Shoreditch from his fight earnings and was located in Juchau Place, later renamed Larks Row. This location no longer exists. As a property owner he would have had the right to vote. No record has been found to indicate that the property remained in the family after his death.

Thomas was registered in the guild for paviors, where he had to serve a seven year apprenticeship. Guilds, which date back to the 14th century, had charters from the City of London to regulate apprenticeships and oversee the standards of their craftsmen. Paviors first appeared in London in 1276, repairing and cleaning streets and their guild was established in 1479. Today they are known as the Worshipful Company of Paviors and received a Royal Charter in 2004. Members today are involved with all scientific, technical and engineering matters dealing with all paved surfaces from footpaths to airport runways. Thomas never achieved high ranking in the guild and became a journeyman pavior. Working as a pavior, Thomas experienced the growth and dynamics of Georgian London and may have had contact with Poitevin refugees through his father's links.

The quarter in London where young James lived was a low income and hardship area spawning pauperism and crime. At the conclusion of the war with Napoleon, the London James faced had to contend with an influx of soldiers, as well as the setback to commerce and industry and the growth of unemployment. These conditions, especially the irregularity of work, added to the many challenges confronting James' household. As a large poor family they contended with an expanding industrialised London, worsening slum conditions, continuing urban poverty, increasingly crowded housing, deteriorating social conditions, sanitation and public health problems, and little or no educational opportunity. Occasionally James would have observed violence and public disorder by groups of workers, especially poor weavers, protesting conditions and injustices.

Children in his neighbourhood, from the age of six, worked and rarely undertook schooling. He had also the threat of deadly epidemics, such as cholera, influenza, small pox, measles, scarlet fever and typhus, which could strike at any moment. By being born into a growing family hobbled by the lack of income and adverse living conditions, James, with no or little education, was on the margin of society and his adult horizon promised little. His community was likened to a pandemonium of misery. Like many boys of his time and in his district, he would have needed to find work in the streets, securing a penny for menial tasks. Often he would have been competing with homeless street children who also sought menial work and who stooped to petty crime to alleviate their misery and poverty.

Historical accounts of his environs vividly capture the conditions facing James and his family. The area and many adjoining neighbourhoods had developed into slums, where ordinary houses where subdivided to accommodate multiple tenants. Landlords spent little on maintenance and many tenants were forced to live chicken-coop style. Dwellings were dilapidated and mostly shabby tenements. Large families crowded into one or two rented rooms facing narrow alleys, cul – de-sacs, rows, lanes, courts and streets. Much of the housing was described as unhygienic, dirty, musty, degraded, gloomy, dark, damp and miserable.

Observers described such conditions as ripe for villainy. Foul air and fog served to emphasise the pall of surroundings. Whole families also occupied cellars and garrets and windows were often lined with paper. Those who were better off lived in the main rooms of the tenements. Access to higher floors was afforded by ladders. Outside, dwellings faced rotting refuse, sewerage and dirt piles which were often left uncollected for long periods. A public privy and water pipe stand may have been the only public amenity. Some thoroughfares were kept clean and some dwellings had space out front which was regularly swept and cleaned. Some streets had cookhouses, eating houses, public houses, garment vendors, and shops.

James would not recognise his neighbourhood today which is being rapidly transformed by fashionable multi storey office and residential buildings and only vestiges of Victorian Shoreditch and Bethnal Green are still recognisable. The street where he was raised has lost most of its early Victorian housing and perhaps only one or two buildings remain of James' period. Today, new style living precludes the kind of street and social interaction experienced by James. Anonymity and social isolation are a common result of apartments in new residential Shoreditch, where a middle class of singles and small families confront employment conditions demanding increasing time commitments. Adjacent neighbourhoods are also transforming, whilst still retaining lower standard housing occupied by immigrant groups from Asia, Africa and the Middle East.

James' childhood experience included the ebb and flow of street commerce, where sellers and traders moved through his district marketing their wares and services. Outside his home or in his quarter, a regular parade of sellers would pass throughout the day. There would be sweeps, dustmen, rag-pickers, milkmen, costermongers, fishmongers, boys taking orders for bakers and butchers, pedlars offering items from tinware to crockery to firewood, tinkers, knife grinders and paper boys. Many traded second-hand clothes, and scavenging for metal, rags and bones by children, was a common sight. The presence of these sellers may have reminded James of how straitened his family was, as they struggled to buy basic food and clothing for their growing household. And this would be more felt given that their neighbourhood also had some wealth generated by nearby business firms, including clothiers, brewers, drapers, haber-dashers, confectioners, tailors and chandlers.

It is not known whether James and his family were aware of their distant Poitou forbears and that his surname had Poitevin origins and had different versions of its spelling. Possibly, he would have had some inkling of French con-nections from stories passed on from his father, especially stories about Charles. No accounts exist of communications between France and England.

James, his family and relatives continued their links with the Anglican faith and lived in the areas of Spitalfields, Shoreditch and Bethnal Green. Most of the male Juchaus worked in menial jobs including gardeners, hawkers, coach-men, paviors, labourers, woodcutters, costermongers, box makers, bargemen, drapers, and messengers as well as work in more skilled jobs in tailoring, fan making, and ivory carving. Female Juchaus mostly married and few worked outside the home. Those who worked found themselves working in domestic service, whilst others took on jobs as laundresses, hawkers, seamstresses, stall-keepers, cooks and willow weavers.

Around him he would have observed the changing fortunes of the weaving industry, where weavers were often forced to seek income by becoming street hawkers. Thousands of weavers became unemployed as the industry struggled with the increasing imported and cheaper silk cloth. As James entered his 13th year he would have been struck by the decline of the local silk-weaving industry and the large number of weavers forced into the poor house and seeking relief from the parish.

Indebtedness, poverty and insolvency continued to be experienced throughout James' parish and served to reinforce the atmosphere of struggle and gloom, which typified many neighbourhoods. And these conditions were exacerbated by the continuing inflow of unskilled labour, mostly destitute and poor, from the regions and abroad, generating more social and health issues. His parish was caught in a web of pauperism and inhumanity according to some observers.

James' life map, by the time he had reached 12 years of age, would have predicted his journey as a young teenager. A pathway to a comfortable life was unlikely. But a life, similar to that his parents had experienced, was in the offing. Pressure also by his family to find income meant that he was probably tempted to dabble in petty property crime if he was to bring more money to a fragile household economy. His neighbourhood had many criminal gangs involved in theft and chicanery. This crime was slowly addressed by authorities introducing a number of Acts on vagrancy, trespassing and policing in the 1820s, increasing the probability of felons being caught and convicted.

Poor children, mostly boys, were involved in petty theft and were able to get a penny or two by selling the stolen goods to costermongers and flash houses, which received stolen goods. James and his peers would have been exposed to the ways of petty theft, including pick pocketing and shoplifting. As well he would have observed the growing presence of adult gangs, who looted and stole from merchants and traders. In 1829 James entered the world of petty crime.

James, an illiterate errand boy and gardener, came to notice in court records, on the November 27th 1829. They revealed that, while in a haberdashery, he was caught by a shop assistant, Robert White, putting ribbon in his bag. He was then arrested by a police officer, Thomas Shapwell, for shoplifting a roll of ribbon (18 yards and valued at 8 shillings) from Hall's haberdashery in Bishopsgate Street. This form of stealing was known then as "canting the dobbin".

His admission record for Newgate Prison (November 28, 1829) revealed that he was 4'7" (140 cms) tall, of fair complexion, brown hair, grey eyes, stout build and residing in Spitalfields. He was put in crowded cells with hardened prisoners, and likely endured the deprivations, the squalor and the predations of seasoned adult criminals. His fellow inmates, because Newgate was a holding prison, were awaiting trial, transportation or execution. The dirt, vermin and congestion, together with the presence of deranged and drunken inmates, generated appalling conditions. Descriptions of Newgate also mention the stench, cruelty, the abject state of hygiene and clothing as well as the presence of diseases.

How James navigated his time there is hard to imagine. He would have been toughened by his street life in his neighbourhood lanes and alleyways. His possible contacts there with petty criminals and links with networks of juvenile delinquents, also may have prepared him to weather the atrocious conditions of Newgate.

He appeared for trial in the Old Bailey Sessions on December 3rd 1829 when, without legal and family representation, he was sentenced to seven years transportation. His defence was that the ribbon had fallen into his bag. Under this sentence, he was to be sent abroad as punishment, but also to be given an opportunity to reform through assigned work and, if appropriate, an apprenticeship. Despite James having had no previous convictions, there appears to have been no consideration of leniency given to him. No member of his family petitioned the Secretary of State for mercy. There was no record of contact with his family before and after sentencing. It was reported in this time that many families whether through indifference, embarrassment or disassociation, never attempted to contact or to keep a link with their incarcerated offspring.

During this time opinions on the treatment of juvenile criminals were divided and ranged across a mix of punishment, containment and restitution arguments. James was sent to be punished, but also to have a restoration opportunity through training and apprenticeship. The opportunity to undertake training to equip him for a future life after serving his time resonated with the enlightened restitution policies of the first colonial governor of NSW, Arthur Phillip, who made provisions to reform First Fleet convicts during their sentence period.

James was transferred to Chatham onto the juvenile prison hulk, Euryalus, on December 16, 1829, to await transportation. Juvenile hulks for males first appeared in 1824. At Chatham, he joined around 380 juvenile offenders whose ages ranged from 9 to 18 years. He endured squalid and cramped conditions, harsh diets, tough labour and abysmal sanitation standards. He would have faced bullying, as well as contending with fellow inmates, many of whom were

JAMES JUCHAU *was indicted for stealing , on the 27th of November, 18 yards of ribbon, value 8s., the goods of Thomas Hall.*

ROBERT WHITE. *I am servant to Thomas Hall, a haberdasher, of Bishopsgate-street. On the 27th of November, about seven o'clock in the evening, the prisoner came in, and asked for a pair of black kid gloves. I was behind some calicoes in the window, and the moment the lad turned around to get the gloves, I saw the prisoner take a piece of ribbon off the counter and put it in his bag – he did not offer to buy it; I came out, and secured him.*

Cross-examined by MR. PHILLIPS. Q. *Who was in the shop besides you? A. We have about five shopmen; it is a large shop – I believe he was the only customer; I never prosecuted anybody before – I have not seen his father – I do not know what the other shopmen were doing – I am certain the ribbon did not drop off the counter; there is a bar to prevent that.*

(Property produced and sworn to.)

THOMAS SHAPWELL. *I am an office. I was sent for, and found this piece of ribbon in the prisoner's bag – he had got 3s.2d.*

Prisoner's Defence. *It fell into my bag.*

GUILTY. Aged 14. *– Transported for Seven Years.*

suffering foetal alcohol syndrome and depression. Most of his companions would be transported when they reached 15 years.

They faced a strict daily routine of bathing, exercise, prayers, and work, which involved making clothes for the prison service. If he was lucky he would have had his hammock on the upper deck, which was reserved for first time convictions. Boys were punished for transgressions and punishment involved birching, solitary confinement and reduced rations. James was to be one of the 2500 boys passing through the juvenile hulk system which was finally stopped in 1843.

The reaction of James to the prospect of being removed to the colony of NSW is not known. Records of interviews with juveniles like James revealed that many were looking forward to getting away and that a return to their home community after serving time was not always contemplated. There was no record of health problems, punishments or misdemeanours during his five month stay on the Euryalus. Perhaps his upbringing had fortified his spirit, giving him the strength of character to bide his time and avoid being crushed by incarceration.

As James was transferred to his ship, he must have had thoughts and feelings about leaving England and his family. Did shame and guilt flood his mind when thinking of his circumstances and family? How much anxiety did he experience and did the loss of family connection loom large in his thoughts? What amount of emotional strain and fear was generated, as he contemplated shipboard life and his destination? In imagining his future, what information would he have had to guide him? One can only guess what he might have known about the colony and his new homeland. When transferred to his transport ship around May 19th 1830, did he feel sadness and regret and think that possibly this might be the last time he would experience the sights, sounds and smells of London? Did the character and strength which enabled him to weather his juvenile experiences and incarceration fortify him for the journey to a new life?

Chapter 6
James in Colonial NSW

James left London (Sheerness) in June 1830 on the convict transport, *Lord Melville*, captained by Master Browne. This ship was built in Quebec in 1825 and had already transported one load of convicts to NSW in 1829. On the 1830 voyage, it carried 176 male convicts, whose ages ranged from 14 to 60, and reached Sydney on October 21st 1830, recording a sailing time of 137 days to cover the sailing distance of 16,000 miles.

His fellow convicts included robbers, house breakers, shop-lifters, fraud cheats, pick pockets and fowl, sheep and horse stealers. Some had life sentences and a few were married. The majority had been involved in petty crime and were under 30 years old. There was no indication that juveniles were segregated from adult convicts. The ship's record revealed that James was aged 15 years, 4'8" (142 cms) tall, of freckled and pock-pitted complexion, brown hair and hazel eyes. At this time, adult convicts were on average 5'3" (160 cms) tall.

Conditions of the voyages out were an improvement on those of the early transports. The convicts had access to a surgeon and the ship was subject to regular hygiene checks. The standard convict rations in his mess included bread, flour, meat, rice, peas and oats, as well as comfort items including lemon juice, sugar and soap and items for fumigation including brimstone, tar and vinegar. Leg irons were not used to manage convicts. The Master's report on the voyage indicated it was unexceptional. Guards for the ship came from a detachment of the 17th Regiment.

There are no personal diaries or records known to exist of the ship's voyage, daily life and conditions on board. From a review of colonial and ship records, it appears that James may have encountered some of these fellow transportees during his time later, as an assigned convict and when he became a free man. It is not known whether he saw his fellow felons as worthy future companions. Did he see his ultimate salvation by distancing himself from the values and mores of felons, and setting out on a pathway where he could uphold his privacy and pursue economic independence?

Accounts of similar voyages of his time suggest that James would have shared a six foot square berth of four convicts on a poorly ventilated deck. Cramped, gloomy, and damp conditions together with foul air made life below decks tough, together with odours from the waste buckets and the stench of the bilge. No deaths were recorded by the ship's surgeon and for a four month voyage, the absence of serious medical and health events was noteworthy. Nevertheless he would have been tested by on-board social conditions where bullying, harassment and cruelty were common, as well as enduring the restrictions on normal life. He would have had to overcome sea-sickness, as well as managing his personal hygiene requirements and maintaining a mental and physical toughness to weather on board conditions and life. Menial tasks, such as swabbing, laundering and scrubbing would have to be routinely done.

Voyages such as the one James experienced brought a regime of order, which made travel tedious, exacerbated by the constraints and prohibitions accompanying convict transportation. He was part of the social freight, negotiating his place and establishing a persona to ensure his physical and emotional survival amongst a mixed assortment of felons. While aspects of the journey were isolating, there were opportunities to socialise and gain friendships. The journey gave James an opportunity to forge a new identity and interactions with crew and soldiers gave more insights into a regulated life. During the journey, shipboard discussions perhaps may have given James other views about prospects and options for a life in the colony.

No personal account exists of James imprisonment and transportation. A curtain of silence was drawn on this part of his life. In later family oral accounts of his life from his grandchildren, this part of his history became a blank page for his descendants. If he told his children, they did not relay this to their children. Like many convicts, he was no doubt loath to acknowledge and record his convict heritage and early life as a felon. Perhaps he was like many successful colonialists, who drew a line across their previous history. Reinforcing this is the fact that many males of that period and even of the present era often do not reveal past events of trauma and personal degradation. As late as 1950, there was no written reference or acknowledgement in family stories of this convict heritage. His Old Bailey sentence record and hulk experience were first unearthed in 2003.

On October 25th 1830, James attended the ship's muster, conducted by the Colonial Secretary. James was assigned to a juvenile barracks on November 2nd 1830. He found himself in Carters' Barracks (corner Devonshire and George Streets), which was designed to house up to 100 boy convicts. There, he was to undertake apprentice training, receive rudimentary education and religious instruction. This institution (originally known as Carters' House of Correction) was set up by Governor Macquarie to be an industrial reformatory for boys. It was hoped that, in time, the reformed and trained juveniles would become valuable additions to the skilled labour supply in the colony.

Drawing Carters' Barracks

Opened in 1820, Carters' Barracks was the first colonial building that separated convict boys from adult male convicts. It had previously only housed adult convicts working as brick makers and carters. Juvenile boys were assigned to undertake training and instruction to prepare them for work in the settlement. A high wall separated juvenile and adult convicts. The carters looked after horses, harnesses and carts. The Barracks had a treadmill, which was often worked by convicts as a form of punishment.

Until 1820, boy convicts in Sydney had not been confined separately and lived among other convicts, working as labourers or servants, while a few were assigned as apprentices. In Tasmania convicted juveniles had no separate living quarters. For example, in the late 1820s in Tasmania, they were assigned to Macquarie Harbour and in 1830 they were sent to Port Arthur. Girl convicts were assigned as servants to settlers or employed in female factories.

Carters' Barracks for boys closed in 1834 and from 1835 all boy convicts were transported to Point Puer ("puer" being the Latin word for "boy") in Port Arthur, Tasmania, which had become a penal Station in 1830. At Point Puer, a purpose built institution for juveniles was established in 1834. Many observers noted that conditions and training at Point Puer were considerably inferior to those at Carters' Barracks. By 1847 the Barracks had been demolished and its equipment distributed for other uses. The Barracks occupied the site where the present precinct of Central Railway sits.

James' new town, Sydney, was expanding through maritime linkages, harbour industrial life, new settlers and overseas trade. He would have seen the results of Macquarie's building program, the evolving streetscape, settler cottages, shops, crowded wharves, changes in vegetation and ever present sandstone backdrop. He experienced the impact of Governor Darling's administration and the emerging civic life of the 37,000 predominantly male inhabitants of Sydney. Amongst them were convicts in government employ, settlers, Ticket of Leave men, emancipists and soldiers. Workers were reportedly paid well and fresh food was widely available.

Routines, provisions, technical and religious instruction at Carters gave James a chance to rehabilitate. Life was highly structured and regimented. Food and clothing rations, together with a strict hygiene system, ensured that the health and welfare of the boys had a sound foundation. The mixture of vocational and religious schooling under a strict regimen of discipline and learning tasks gave James a foundation from which to elevate his outlook, as well as supplying skills to navigate through the penal system and join society as a productive citizen. Importantly, he learnt the rudiments of reading and writing. It was claimed that many boys were transformed, morally and socially, and prepared to take on life as responsible citizens.

His apprenticeship was completed in October 1832 when he gained a qualification in harness making (Div. 2, 1st Class). At this time, there were 57 boys at the barracks. During his stay he was admitted to hospital twice and served two days in solitary confinement for fighting. Some of his peers failed to finish their trade. Some who had served their time, later regressed and resumed a career of villainy. There were others who absconded and, if they reoffended, found themselves placed into a convict labour pool or subjected to transportation to places like Port Macquarie in northern NSW.

James was able to manage the pressures of barrack life, contending with the discipline of his supervisors, as well coping with his peers, many of whom tried to impose their own authority on the young and weak and subject them to bullying and intimidation. Outsiders observed that many of the boys were better schooled and trained to a level which, given their backgrounds, could never have been envisaged in England.

After three years of apprenticeship, boys were normally assigned to a settler. James remained at the Barracks until July 1833, when he was assigned to Robert Scott at Glendon, an estate in the lower Hunter Valley between Maitland and Singleton. Apprentices from Carters' were highly sought after by settlers, because the government guaranteed a period of their service. They could supply useful skills as well as having experienced the discipline of supervised work. Records showed that the demand from settlers for apprentices well exceeded the supply.

In his time at the Barracks James may have formed the seed of an idea of what to do when his sentence was completed. He would have seen many examples in town life, where former convicts successfully pursued employment in the emerging colonial economy and a new urban collective of diverse groups. In 1831 he saw the departure of Governor Ralph Darling and the arrival of the new Governor, Richard Bourke. Perhaps he saw, despite colonial and military restrictions, a life of opportunity and the chance to gain a new persona. He may have appreciated his good fortune to have had an opportunity to gain training and education which would support him in his future pursuits.

At Glendon, he joined 60 other workers (smithies, ploughmen, carpenters, cattlemen, dairymen) to work as a saddler and harness maker. Workers' efforts to build the Scotts' (Robert and Helenus) 4000 acre estate, ten miles from the present-day town of Singleton, were widely praised at the time. The workers were housed in huts, apart from the main house. Glendon was becoming famous as a colonial horse stud, and by 1833 had 300 horses. Many of the horses became foundation stock for the development of thoroughbred breeding. They featured in colonial racecourse meetings throughout the Hunter Valley. The Scotts' original homestead remains to this day, although it is presently unoccupied.

As a skilled assigned convict, James enjoyed the basic rations of flour, beef, milk and tobacco, as well as tea and sugar. Clothes, shoes and cooking utensils were supplied. He may have been rewarded also with an allowance of spirits and money, which may also have been supplemented by earnings for work done for neighbouring farms. He would work from sunrise to sunset with a lunch break. The annual cost of maintaining a convict at this time was around seventeen pounds. His diet and life were arguably superior to those of his London peer group. Comparative research data on convict health, nutrition and life expectancy suggest that James would have been considerably better off than his family, peers and neighbours back in the East End of London.

What would James have made of this rural community? The contrast between London and the lower Hunter would have been striking. Large tracts of bush, cleared land, aboriginal encampments, the fauna and flora would all have impressed. The Hunter River and its feeder streams may not have been an arcadia, but its potential for successful agriculture would have been apparent. At this stage, did he ponder a future as a farmer or did he see the opportunity to become employed in one of the new towns opening up in the upper Hunter region?

Certainly the pulses of commerce and agriculture were apparent in the Hunter, as farmers and business people were registering success in the new lower Hunter settlements on the Paterson, Patrick and Wallis plains, where freed convicts and new settlers had taken up land assigned by colonial governors. Around Patrick Plains James would have encountered a number of his fellow transportees from the Lord Melville, who were assigned to work on farms there. Agriculture, forestry and coal mining were becoming the economic drivers of the region and were benefited by sea and river transport which now gave regular links to Sydney. Important service towns, including Morpeth, Maitland and Singleton, all shared this economic growth.

While still at Glendon, James received his Ticket of Leave on July 7th 1835, allowing him to leave the employ of his assigned master, to be free of government labour requirements and to work in the district of Maitland. The ticket, subject to annual review, could be withdrawn by local constables or magistrates, if he broke leave conditions or the law. He was free to be self-employed. There is no record of other employment with this ticket. He must have been well regarded by his master to secure his ticket. His master, who had a tough reputation, had been known to collude with rural magistrates to deny granting the ticket to retain a cheap labour source. It was possible that James continued to work with Scott until he was emancipated.

His Certificate of Freedom, granted in April, 1837, gave him the rights of a free settler. In 1837 it is recorded that he was 5'3,3/4" (162 cms) tall, freckled and of pale complexion, with brown hair and grey eyes, a scar on the inside of his left wrist, and a wart on the third finger of his left hand. He would now be classified as part of a colonial group, referred to as *emancipists*. It was ironical that he gained freedom in the year that Governor Bourke announced that convicts were not to be assigned to private employers. And would he have rejoiced that this was the year Victoria became Queen? The date he left Glendon is not recorded, but a later reference indicated that he got to Scone sometime in 1839. A search of the Scott archives in the NSW State Library does not show movements and departure of their assigned convict labour.

In the year 1837, what did the 22 year old James make of his lot and prospects and what did he know about his family activity back in the East End? Did he know of the development of the Pages River Valley, where he was to ultimately settle and that a road, the Great North Road from Singleton, had reached the Valley by 1833? He may have heard that many of his convict shipmates had been assigned to farms in the Scone district and the Pages River Valley and perhaps they and others, through the grapevine, had given reports about the potential of the districts. His thinking may have been shaped by the good farming seasons and prosperity of the region, experienced between 1830 and 1836. He may have also heard reports of the dangers of droughts, which the region had previously experienced in 1828-29.

No records exist to give a hint of his disposition and outlook. Indirectly, and on the evidence from his later life, he must have had a gritty, determined and entrepreneurial streak to surmount his convict "blemish" and to embark on building a life in an unsettled and challenging region of the Upper Hunter Valley, where his deeds, not his antecedence, would allow him to build a reputation as an industrious and reputable citizen. Perhaps this was echoed earlier in his commitment and loyalty to the operations of Scotts, where his abilities and usefulness gave him an untroubled journey as an assigned and then a Ticket of Leave convict.

His views about religion and colonial authorities remain unknown. There are indirect clues from his later involvement in his community, where he supported Anglican

Church development and took on civic roles in advancing schooling and township development. He was an upholder of the Anglican faith and his contributions to civic affairs indicated that he had respect for the colonial administration. He clearly had an entrepreneurial spirit, as evidenced by his building of a successful retail business and investing in town property.

Perhaps he possessed the Huguenot spirit which is claimed to have the hallmarks of self-reliance, industriousness and independence. Or was he simply adopting the prevailing values of his NSW colonial society, noted for being individualistic, acquisitive and enterprising? And did he reflect later, that he was one of a small group who had emerged from the 80,000 convicts transported to NSW to go on to become important contributors to the creation and development of townships in rural NSW?

Map of NSW

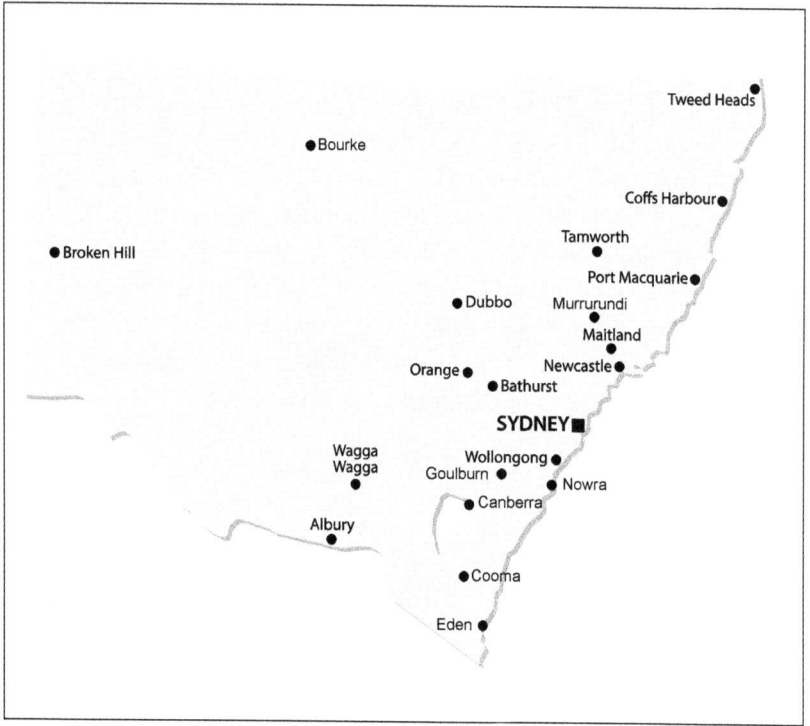

Chapter 7
James in Murrurundi

By 1840, James is next recorded in the Upper Hunter Valley,living and working in the village of Scone, formerly named Invermein. He was employed as a saddler in Thomas Dangar's store. There is no account of when he left Glendon. Records, however, do show that Dangar had business dealings with the Scotts and this may have given James knowledge about Scone and its prospects and a link to employment there. As well, he knew that many of his companions on the ship were working in the Scone district, where many had received their Ticket of Leave.

The town was first surveyed in 1836 and named Invermein. It was situated on the main stock route to the north and north-west tablelands. In1838, it was renamed Scone. By 1840, a village consisting of huts, stores, inns and a church, had been established. The town's population was small, around 60 people, and it is not clear what regard free settlers and storekeepers had for former convicts and whether Scone's social structure was inclusive. The settlement was a critical service centre, supporting the opening up of agriculture and allowing more development in the Upper Hunter region.

James came to public notice there on December 20th 1840, when he, with a fellow employee, John Graham, fled from a robbery in Dangar's store. They raised the alarm with the local blacksmith. Tragically he saw Graham fatally shot by the robbers, known as the Jewboy Gang. James and others were taken prisoners by the gang, who proceeded to hold up the store and the nearby inn, the St. Aubins Arms.

The gang was captured the next day at Doughboy Hollow at Ardglen. James gave evidence at the trial to convict the robbers and murderers. The gang, led by a transported felon, Ed Davis, had become notorious for a number of robberies committed in the Hunter Valley. Following conviction the gang were hanged in Sydney in 1841.

These events may have caused James to reflect on his past. Here he is a free man showing courage to report a robbery and give evidence at a court. It was only 11 years earlier in December when he was arrested for robbery himself. And it was the year 1840 that saw the end of transportation to NSW. The month of December and 1840 would be significant dates in James' life. His actions, as well as his employment may have given James a chance to demonstrate to his community that he was a worthy citizen, and his past was becoming somewhat irrelevant for judging his character.

On July 22nd 1841, James married Elizabeth Delve in the courthouse in Scone.

Elizabeth was born in1820 in Loxhore, North Devon and was the daughter of James Delve and Anne Delve, who were married in Loxhore in 1818. James Delve was the village blacksmith and the ruins of his premises still remain in Loxhore today. Elizabeth was the first born of six siblings. She received some education and worked as a domestic servant in the Loxhore district and probably in the nearby Devon market town of Barnstaple. The town also had a Huguenot link. Many Huguenots had settled there permanently and a strong presence emerged in the 18th century. They ran business firms and many became civic leaders.

The scattered village of Loxhore, comprising Lower Loxhore, Loxhore Cott and Loxhore Town, depended largely on agriculture, which supported a population of 300 in Elizabeth's time. In nearby Barnstaple, she would have

Photos Elizabeth and James

seen many advertisements by packet shipping companies for rural workers and domestic servants to emigrate to NSW. Advertisements for young single women, between the ages of 18 and 30, had first appeared in 1833, following initiatives to increase the supply of female labour to the colony. The advertisements outlined fares (typically 20 pounds for an unassisted single female passenger), voyage conditions, clothing requirements for passengers and the victualling arrangements for the voyage. The fare represented about the average annual wage of a male agricultural labourer working in Southern England. Single females had to furnish "unquestionable" testimonials and to be of "exceptional character". The advertisements emphasised that emigrants would be free agents when they arrived in Sydney.

Elizabeth left England on 11th October, 1840 and arrived in Sydney on February 1st 1841, on the ship *Posthumous*. It carried general cargo, 24 cabin passengers, 13 steerage passengers and 18 crew members. She arrived in the transforming and expanding colony of NSW, which was advantaged by the arrival of an increasing number of free settlers. Its population was around 118,000. She travelled as a steerage passenger, where she shared a communal dormitory located between decks, with two tiers of bunks and a dining table. Ventilation and hygiene problems were encountered. Smells of insanitary conditions would have been ever present, together with fumigants, which were added to charcoal burners to counter the fetid air below decks. The ship had sailed from the Downs via Bahia, Brazil, and the voyage took three and a half months. Coincidentally, the ship also carried horses for the Scotts, James' first masters.

As a domestic servant, Elizabeth was like most migrant unmarried women in the colony, where seven out of ten were domestic or farm servants. Her voyage was uneventful and she arrived in Sydney in good health. Soon after arrival, she made her way to Scone to work in domestic service.

It is not clear whether Elizabeth had responded to those advertisements in Barnstaple, for women to work as domestics in the colony, or whether she was in the employ of a Mrs Darby, who was a cabin passenger on the *Posthumous*, and who may have gone to live in the Scone area. There is no record in colonial passenger or transport lists of Elizabeth's move from Sydney to Scone. In all likelihood, she would have travelled by boat from Sydney to Morpeth, before travelling on foot or by wagon from Maitland to Scone via Singleton and Muswellbrook. These settlements were linked by tracks and stock routes and a horse rider might take two days to travel from Maitland to Scone.

Within two months of arriving, Elizabeth had received the Governor's permission to marry Michael Burrows, a Ticket of Leave holder. In a letter from a district resident, Elizabeth is described as a cherry-cheeked handsome English girl. The marriage did not take place, since Burrows had committed an offence and was given a 12 months sentence in irons. Three months later she married James. The minister, the reverend John Morse, was the Anglican Chaplain of Scone described by many as obese, dumpy and ill-natured, and was said to view Methodists as heretics capable of sedition.

There are no diaries or letters of Elizabeth. Her willingness to marry quickly and settle in a new country is clear. Her choices of marriage partners and employment may have been limited by the small population in the district, but certainly she would have been aware that single women were eagerly sought for marriage in a colony long suffering a shortage of women. Around her, she would have witnessed many women marrying, building a family and providing security for a challenging future. Writers have speculated that many marriages in the colony were opportunistic and the element of romance may not have been to the fore. Marriages often took place within six months of first meetings. Men normally initiated the proposal and the average age of marriage for women was normally around 20 to22 years. The average age for men was around 25 to 27 years.

Elizabeth, the 22 year old Devonshire lass, now had the chance to start and build a family life in a pioneering rural setting. Her roots in agricultural and village life in Loxhore may have given her confidence to face the challenges of raising a family and facing life in a remote rural district, subject to some extreme rhythms of nature, shifting populations and volatile agricultural markets.

Were the key elements that bound Elizabeth and James in marriage based on their backgrounds and the prospect of the economic benefits flowing from a family household? Families were regarded as critical institutions in the expanding colony. They gave critical support to frontier life, as well as becoming community keystones in new settlements. The colonial family was often seen as the only rural institution able to provide the necessary range of support for health, nurturing, welfare and education. James and Elizabeth were now cast as a pioneer couple, destined to form a lifelong working friendship. Their hopes would be to raise a family and to become part of the social fabric of a new rural township in NSW.

James and Elizabeth would have heard of the country north of Scone which was opening up for new settlement, as a result of exploration in 1824. Pioneering work in the 1830s in the upper Hunter around the Pages River Valley and surrounding districts brought about permanent settlement.

James may have been encouraged by possible contact with a former young shipmate, convict John Small, who had been assigned to a farm in the valley. They knew that they would have to buy their own land, since the Government had stopped allocating free land grants to emancipists in 1825. James and Elizabeth moved to the valley in 1842 to set up a business in a river settlement known as Buttontown. This settlement was located on a property, Mabyn Vale, owned by Charles Button, hence the name of the settlement. Their move may have also been influenced by James' former employer, Thomas Dangar, who opened an inn and stores at Pages River. The journey from Scone covered 25 miles (40km.) and followed rough tracks and stock routes. There is no trace of Buttontown today.

The district and valley were pioneered in 1829 by William Warland, who was joined by Irishman Peter Haydon and later his brother Thomas Haydon. The valley and the Pages River, which originates in the Liverpool Range, would, under normal conditions have indicated good prospects for agriculture. Warland had first settled south of Murrurundi, near the present village of Blandford, which took its name from a town in Dorset, where Warland was educated. John Small, a young shipmate of James, had been assigned initially to Warland and then to Haydon. There is no record of James meeting him when he arrived. The area also benefited from the energies of key settlers, including Peter Brodie. All were now part of the many enterprising migrants, who settled the Upper Hunter Valley, seeking a living and a new life by securing property along and around the Pages River.

By 1837, an informal settlement had emerged on the Pages River around a crossing or ford-site, and where a post office was established. The settlement at this time was known as Pages River or The Page. The presence of a reliable place for provisioning and communication provided the basis for a frontier village to emerge. Initially it suffered from disorder and drunken behaviour, but over time civil order prevailed, encouraging more squatters, small traders and families to settle. It had also become a favoured camping place for teamsters following a bullock track to the Liverpool Range to the north. It became a place of settlement where new arrivals supplied the ingredients for township development.

Local aborigines called the area "Murrumdoorandi" believed to mean "the meeting place of the five fingers" referring to the backdrop of five peaks surrounding the vicinity of the settlement. The tribal group in the district was known as the Wanaruah or Wonnarua. Their tribal territory stretched from the Liverpool Ranges in the north, Wollombi in the south, Merriwa in the west and to the fringes of the Barrington Tops to the east. Their distribution and population shrank over the 19th century and by 1890 the Singleton area became the location where most Hunter remnant groups were to be found. Their totem was the wedge-tailed eagle.

Sporadic clashes occurred between settlers and aborigines. James had reported in the Maitland Mercury that in the early 1840s, as many as 200 aborigines had camped along the river flat and regularly held corroborees. By 1860, their only local presence was in a small group at Scone. There was no record of aboriginal presence in the district by 1890. Settler activity accelerated the decline of the aboriginal population. Both the Hunter Valley and the Liverpool Ranges to the north harboured an assortment of settlers and former convicts, who visited settlements for supplies and contributed to village drunkenness and disorder. This together with the pressures of settlement growth and accompanying European social conditions heralded the decline and disappearance of aboriginal activity around the river flats of the Upper Hunter.

On a Pages River settlement block acquired from Peter Brodie, Thomas Haydon developed a private town, Haydonton, which adjoined the newly formed (1840) government township of Murrurundi. The plan for the government town was set down in 1839, as the village of "Murrurunda". The main thoroughfare for the two towns was called Mayne Street after Haydon's friend, Captain Mayne. The twin towns, however, operated as one community, pursuing common civic and social goals and sharing community amenities. However each town had separate post and later telegraph offices, which only became a single operation in 1913.

These two adjoining townships were the last settlements of the Upper Hunter lying close to the foot of the Liverpool Ranges. They became the gateway to the Northern Tablelands. Haydonton became a model for private town development in the colony. By 1913 however, the township of Haydonton had lost its separate identity and was deleted from government listings of NSW settlement sites. To some locals it became known then as South Murrurundi.

James transferred their business from Buttontown to Haydonton in 1842. A store and residence were built on land (Deeds Lot 19.Section 2, Haydonton) in Mayne Street next to the White Hart Inn, which continues to trade today. The building was a low, detached skillion-roofed construction, comprising a store, initially for harness making, and two rooms. It was reported that he moved his trading stock from Buttontown to Haydonton in a wheelbarrow. In an interview (*Maitland Mercury*, Jan. 4th 1896) James, then 82 years old, recalled his early days. He mentioned Buttontown, a mile down river from Haydonton. Settlements were linked by pathways zigzagging through the bush. He said every one walked, since horses were scarce. There was only a one horse gig available and it was located at Scone.

The decade of the 1840s brought tough economic conditions, following a financial downturn, droughts and falling wool prices. In 1843 wool, which had sold for 25 pence per pound in 1836, dropped to 12 pence per pound. Fat cattle, which had sold for 7 pounds per head in 1841, fetched 3 pounds. James was forced to supplement his income by working as an overseer on Haydon's property at Bloomfield (Blandford), as well as leasing land there to operate as a tenant farmer. In 1841 the Pages River ceased to flow, forcing settlers to go elsewhere to collect water.

Over the period 1841-46, James kept the business running and sold off his farm tenancy in 1846. This gave him more resources, enabling him to survive a further drought in 1847. The drought and a plague of flies in 1847 continued to make life difficult and the plague brought universal misery to humans and animals alike. By 1848, James was able to get his business into good order, expanding into a general store and to also purchase building sites in Haydonton. On some sites, he built small cottages, some of which were rented.

The settlements were growing, with 22 houses in Haydonton, and 11 in Murrurundi. Growth was underpinned by government outpost services including a Petty Sessions court in 1843 and a school in 1849. Being sited on the main road (now the New England Highway) to the Tablelands meant that both towns benefited from the growing passing trade. Accommodation was provided by boarding houses and hotels, Travellers' Home and the Woolpack Inn in Murrurundi, and the White Hart Inn in Haydonton. The towns also benefited from a growing community spirit and inclusiveness which contributed to the growth of voluntarism and mutual respect. As well, the towns were strengthened by their cultural mix. English, Irish and Scottish settlers worked cooperatively with emancipists to bring about sustainable settlements.

Involvement with Haydon may have reminded James of his links to the Scotts at Glendon. Thomas Haydon had commercial dealings with the Scotts in the 1840s. Haydon had borrowed money from them and had also bought one of their thoroughbred stallions, *Dover*, which was used for racing and stud purposes. *Dover* won many races at district race meetings. There is little doubt that James would have known of Haydon's dealings and might have presumed that Haydon and the Scotts had exchanged views about him, and perhaps affirming his qualities as a tradesman and citizen.

Thomas Haydon, a liberal Catholic, had also a reputation for tolerance and inclusiveness. He was admired by locals for being free of bigotry. He openly mixed and worked with Anglicans, Presbyterians, ex convicts and Irish labourers. Haydon appeared not to hold prejudices. His knowledge of the previous life of James did not hinder their working relationship in business and community affairs. Haydon's enterprise and inclusiveness give an example of the importance of a key leader and stakeholder in founding colonial settlements. A social chemistry was generated encouraging others to join in establishing viable communities. And it raises the important question of how the destinies of many rural towns may have been doomed, because they lacked the inclusive leadership, perseverance, talents and energies of well – resourced settlers like Thomas Haydon. It appeared that some of the darker sides of colonial life – religious sectarianism and social inequality – had not visited the towns of Haydonton and Murrurundi.

Fictional and historical accounts of the intermingling of former convicts and free settlers in small rural townships

do not always give a clear picture of how relationships operated and were sustained. At one extreme, there were divided
communities where class and origins led to division and at
the other extreme were open and inclusive communities,
where little or no outward prejudices were apparent and
commingling was the rule, not the exception.

In Murrurundi and Haydonton, it appeared that little
social division occurred and the community pulled together
to make them places of permanent settlement. They were
able to confront the climatic, economic, and civic challenges which towns faced in frontier rural NSW. People
there appeared to promote mutuality and to avoid social
division arising from background, wealth, power or status.
Civil manners and civic energy, not background, appeared
to be the criteria for assessing a person's character. It is hard
to conceive that James could have kept his convict past
quiet, given his previous employment in the Hunter and
being blessed or cursed for having an unusual surname.
His energy, skills and civic contributions were to assure his
respectability and acceptance.

Over the period, 1842-50, the family grew with the birth
of two sons, James or Jimmy (1842-1913)) and Charles or
Charly (1844-1923) and two daughters, Sarah (1846-1940)
and Frances or Fanny (1850-1930). All were baptised by visiting Anglican ministers from Scone in the local courthouse,
since the Anglican Church, St Pauls, was not built until 1856.

St Pauls Church was rebuilt in sandstone in 1874. James
had supported the building of the original church by a
donation of 11 pounds, 15 shillings and sixpence – the third
largest donor. He also donated a bell to this church, which
remained until the new church was built. Somehow this bell
was later removed and installed in St Lukes Anglican Church
at Blandford, where it remains to this day. The Blandford

church was built in1879, replacing a wooden building constructed by William Warland. The bell carries James' name and its date 1856. The electoral roll of 1852 registered James as a freeholder of Haydonton.

Unusual of the time, James and Elizabeth had a small number of children. Typically, colonial families had seven to nine children and whilst, often a burden, the large families also became important elements in sustaining a household economy. Two year birth intervals were not unusual for the period. There was no explanation for their small family unit, although their two daughters and two sons all went on to have large families.

While hard economic conditions had confronted the growing family and the settlement, recovery was underway once the half century was reached. They were to face a prosperous decade of the 1850s, where higher prices for wool and livestock were obtained and the growth of industry was registered in the Hunter region. This was boosted by gold discovery on the Peel River near Nundle, bringing new passing trade and commercial opportunities. Better transport was important to settlement life, including regular coach services to Scone and Maitland and the commencement in 1846 of heavy goods shipments from Maitland by horse and bullock wagons. Shipments could be held up from floods and were subject to some pilfering, especially the rum supplies. As well, a twice weekly mail service from Sydney led to more contact with the outside world and more reliable information to the settlers.

James must surely have felt some pride in his progress over the period 1830-50. In twenty years, he had gone from a juvenile convict to a successful business and family man. He had acquired property, and had become a patron of the national school which was the first in the Hunter Valley outside Newcastle. He had overcome his blighted background, pursued the goal of economic independence and gained success in an environment beset with the problems of new town life, unpredictable and damaging climatic conditions and the consequent ups and downs of agriculture. In a way his progress occurred in step with the town's developments and its openness to embrace contributions from across the social divide.

James ran regular store advertisements in the *Maitland Mercury*, promoting his business ethics and the range of merchandise for sale. The style of the advertisements reflected a confident and positive proprietor, proud of his business and his community. He now was a local identity. He had bonds and allegiances with the town through family, business and civic networks. His identity was now interlinked with the identities of Haydonton and Murrurundi. Their histories were now interwoven. He had developed a sense of belonging in his town. He faced no social division, it would seem, and had little likelihood of encountering class division, which was reported to be the experience of some former convicts, was apparently never to be experienced.

The style and manner of his life may have been a reflection of the norms arising from Victorian values and colonial rules, modified by local values. He may have been affected by the rush of energy and opportunism emerging in the district. The demands of an emerging locality, which required special civic interdependence by the founding and pioneering families, were destined to prevail. Like many who were emancipated, the present and future mattered and the past, whilst important in shaping outlooks, lost its significance as identity and purpose took a new tack for sustaining settlement. Respectability came from property ownership, social manners and active civic involvement. Virtue was achieved by deeds not wealth and social background. For James, town life gave a chance to remove the impediments of a former life. Rather than conviction, transportation and assignment, it was civic involvement that would define his life.

James would have noted changes in diets. Conditions were improving and were in stark contrast to the mutton, damper and black tea diet of many rural workers. Tea, sugar and bread were always important to the daily diet, and as horticulture, transport, markets and prices improved, jam, butter, milk, fresh meat and vegetables featured more regularly in the diet of the Juchau household. Ultimately, candlelight would give way to kerosene lamps, the tinder box to matches, the pack horses and bullock drays to the steam train and the meat safe to the ice chest. Beer would surpass brandy, gin and rum as the preferred alcoholic drink, confectionary consumption rose, while tobacco remained the staple drug.

James recognised the importance of newspapers to promote his business. His district was served by the *Maitland Mercury* which, in addition to the pulpit and post office, was an indispensable source of information. It was the vehicle to keep communities close and to strengthen their spirits and uplift their outlook. Some saw *"The Mercury"* as giving a coherent voice to the Hunter Valley development and having an indispensable role in underwriting its culture and prospect.

James witnessed the population growth of his town and district from 52 in 1846 to 600 by 1863. This population increase paralleled that of the colony, which had grown through free emigration, especially during the period 1830-1860. By 1861, Sydney's population was 56,000, while the population for the rest of the colony of NSW was 292,000. Despite the ups and downs of the economy, the district had shown resilience. James would have been bemused perhaps by the anti-transportation meetings that emerged in 1851-52, seeking to end convict transport to the colonies. And what were his views when convict transportation to Eastern Australia finally ended?

James became the enterprising townsman, expanding his store and real estate holdings in Haydonton. He owned several building blocks and his store sold groceries, drapery, saddles, and wine and spirits, all of which he had freighted from Sydney. He engaged in civic affairs and kept his involvement in the Anglican Church where he and his son, James Jnr, were pew holders (1858-1868).

James pushed for improvements in schooling. Because of low standards at the national school, he and others sponsored private tuition in 1854 and removed their children from the school. Until 1878, when a new public school opened, the district families supported private schooling (five operated in 1877) and private tutors.

The Juchau household expanded in December 1856, when Elizabeth's sisters, Susan and Frances with her young son Charles, together with her widowed mother, arrived from Devon to join them. The family had travelled out as cabin passengers on the *La Hogue* together with another Delve, Elizabeth's brother Francis, who remained in Sydney. It is not known whether their passage was paid by James. They came into a district now with a growing population and with a road network extending into the North West Tablelands. Nothing is recorded about their reception or what the circumstances were promoting a journey to Australia. Perhaps the reports of Elizabeth's new found life and her relative affluence encouraged their migration. In 1865 Frances Delve married William Lowndes, a fettler, and together with her young son, Charles, moved to live in Gunnedah.

Town map of Haydonton

PLAN

TOWNSHIP OF **HAYDONTON**

PARISH OF MURRURUNDI   COUNTY OF BRISBANE

Page River

BROOK STREET

MAYNE STREET

ADELAIDE STREET

LIVERPOOL STREET

HAYDON STREET

VICTORIA STREET

POLDING STREET

ALBERT STREET

O'CONNELL STREET

His convict past appeared not to shackle James. His four children all married locally: James Jnr in 1868 to Sarah Williams, daughter of Vincent Williams, a Presbyterian minister; Charles in 1873 to Lucinda Evans, daughter of a local blacksmith; Sarah in 1875 to Thomas Russell, son of a surgeon; and Frances in 1876 to Richard Bourne, son of an overseer with the Australian Agricultural Company. Apart from Charles they all were to settle elsewhere. James Jnr finally settled in Roma, Queensland, Sarah in Goulburn and Frances in Tamworth. James Jnr raised nine children, Charles raised eight, Sarah five and Frances eight. Almost all their children's first names were English perhaps indicating little appreciation of their French background. Charles may have been named after the Frenchman Charles. They adhered to the convention of the time in using well-known English first names.

Prior to these marriages, James went to England in 1863 to visit family (both his parents had died in 1852). He returned in January 1865 on the ship *Nourmahal*. The local paper, *Maitland Mercury*, in 1865, when reporting his return from travel to England, referred to James as "an old colonialist returning to his respected family in the country of his adoption". The trip was perhaps motivated to build links with families and visit his remaining siblings after an absence of 34 years. His trip may have also been business related, although there are no records to support this. Unlike others, who returned to their homeland and generated interest in family members to migrate, no other member of his family ever made it to Australia.

Yet there is some indirect evidence of his convict stigma still possibly impacting his life. By 1868 James had appeared to sever relations with his church, coinciding with the time when the NSW Colonial Governor, Earl of Belmore, made an 1868 official visit to the district, attended the church and stayed overnight at the church rectory. It appears James was excluded from events surrounding the visit. Was James not invited because of his convict background? A letter by his 19 year old daughter, Frances (nicknamed Fanny), to English cousins in 1869, may give a clue. She complains that the family to date had never seen anyone "higher than the local parson".

Correspondence to family in England was encouraged by faster mail services. By sailing ship, letters could take 130 days, but by 1869 this had fallen to 80 days. One letter gave views of the climate and local aborigines of the time. James' daughter, Francis observed that regular rainfall was a rarity and for months the river had had no water. Local aborigines had long moved away. She observed that they were dirty and indolent, and often wore opossum skins. Their clothing was often in bits, never washed and worn until it rotted off. They slept in the open in blankets by their fires. She wrote that she had never seen the sea and ships and had never ventured from town. At this time she was the only one of James children still living at home.

This correspondence and the other rare family letters found, give no hint of what the families in England thought of James' past or whether they were given an edited version of his early life. Perhaps, like many parents with dark pasts, James perhaps gave his children and his surviving relatives edited accounts, which glossed over the convict period or gave a rendering which placed the best spin on the past. Reminiscing about the past may have been a minefield requiring careful selection of what is to be revealed. Again, Victorian values and family customs meant that only some aspects of the past were conveyed and embarrassing periods were avoided or politely evaded when the past was raised.

Unsurprisingly, like many other families with convict fore-bears, a storehouse of secrets had been concealed in this and successive Juchau households and it was not until the middle of the 20th century that his full life story began to emerge.

The continued expansion of the district and township augured well for James and his family. He added a new building for his store in 1869, possibly in anticipation of the arrival of rail. The colonial government decided in 1868 to extend the railway from Singleton to Murrurundi. In 1872 it became a rail terminus, forwarding centre and depot of works to support the rail extension over the Liverpool Ranges to Quirindi. The advent of rail and associated developments, quarries, mills and stores, saw the population in the twin towns grow to 2000 by 1875. In the wool season, it was reported that 40-50 teams of wool carriers were unloading at one time and hundreds were on the road to the terminus. James, as a landlord and storekeeper in Haydonton, benefited from the influx of these workers.

Family ties with English relatives were furthered with regular correspondence. In 1877 James sent five pounds to his second youngest brother, Louis Charles and promised another "tenner" later. Younger son Charles had benefited from the growth of the district. Following employment in Tamworth, he started a business as a baker and general agent in Murrurundi in 1871. His business steadily built in the wake of railway development. His sisters, Frances and Sarah, lost their first babies which brought James the first real tragedy to his family. Charles became the family anchor in the town and James and Elizabeth were enjoying regular visits from his children.

The only family event which may have given James concern in this period was legal proceedings against James

Jnr over livestock and property disputes. Over time James Jnr moved to a number of towns in rural NSW and news reports showed that he often became embroiled in local disputes and controversies wherever he settled. He had a feisty disposition and no doubt generated grief for his father, who had worked hard to gain respect and standing in the Upper Hunter region. James Jnr with some his family finally settled in Queensland running a station first at Surat, "Strathmere" and then Roma, "Hollyrood". He died in 1913.

James, Elizabeth and their son, Charles continued to experience the town's economic ups and downs, especially from 1877, when, no longer a rail terminus and road centre, it suffered a downturn. Economic activity declined following expansion of transport routes to the north and west. In 1878 rail had reached Tamworth, which was fast becoming the principal town of the region. Population declined to 1000. Many shops and an inn were forced to close. James, who had a number of properties rented in Haydonton, also suffered as tenants linked with the railway, moved away. One estimate had the population reduced by two-thirds from its peak in 1875.

An observer noted that the town appeared to be dying and decaying. It did not recover until the late 1880s. It was to suffer again from the recession of 1892 as well as from periodic droughts when the Pages River often ran dry, and was described by a reporter in 1896 as being in a run-down state. The town did not recover until oil shale production commenced there in 1908. The community and the individual psychology of managing drought and its aftermath could be compared to how rural Australia today manages. Resilience and positive demeanours aided survival in both times. In James' case his capital was sunk in the town. His fortunes moved with those of the town and he had no option but to see through all the challenges that the drought posed.

The family also would have observed the absence of the local aboriginal groups, which had disappeared from the district. Frances, in a letter to English cousins had noted this. Other records showed that parts of the upper and lower Hunter Valley also recorded the loss of local aborigines and their absence in a number of towns and districts along the Hunter River.

Charles continued to maintain the Juchau tradition of being involved in civic and community affairs. He and Lucinda raised eight children, the last being born in 1891. He was reported to have a retiring and quiet disposition. In 1890 Murrurundi was gazetted a municipality and he became the first Mayor of Murrurundi, holding office for a total of four years. (His mayoral chain is presently held in Murrurundi's Museum.) Charles was a district coroner and became a colonial magistrate in 1896. For some time he ran a bakery and he may have reflected that 150 years ago his Huguenot forbear, Charles, was also a baker in England. His community involvement included membership of the Race Club, the Masonic Lodge, the School of Arts and Hospital committees. Charles might have been interested to know that a French Juchault, Claude Juchault, is mayor [2016] of the village of Prailles, where he has served many terms. Prailles is close to La Mothe from where Charles' namesake and forbear left for England.

The townships of Haydonton and Murrurundi were hit badly by the financial and monetary crisis in Australia in the 1890s, which saw banks close their doors. Commerce and agriculture were affected. They continued to spiral down-wards and a *Maitland Mercury* reporter in 1896 described the towns as being in "parlous state having been prematurely borne and now a useless expense". Drainage relied on nature, there were no street lamps, and the town had a dirty and dismal appearance.

James continued storekeeping up to his death in 1897. He left an estate of 3246 pounds. Included in the estate were ten properties on Mayne, Liverpool, and Adelaide Streets. Most were largely wood and slab constructions and most were either dilapidated or untenanted. The few that were rented fetched two to five shillings per week. His premises on Mayne Street, next to the present day White Hart Inn consisted of a three-room brick skillion building and an adjoining wooden building comprising a store and two rooms. None of these buildings remain today. At the time of his death, his stock in trade was valued at 42 pounds and nine shillings and included a range of household products as well as hardware and tobacco.

Over his 55 years in Murrurundi, James had built a successful family and business and, through this and his civic contributions, had won respect and high regard for his citizenry and progressive outlook. He had weathered tough times and he had not been handicapped by his convict background.

The Juchau presence in the town continued with Charles and his family. They continued to support James' widow, Elizabeth, who died in March 1902 aged 81 years. She left a large family including 28 grandchildren and nine great grandchildren. With the death of Charles in 1923 and his wife Lucinda in 1929, the Juchau presence in the town ended. The Juchaus were now indelibly sewn into the historical fabric of Murrurundi. James, Elizabeth, Charles and Lucinda were all buried in Murrurundi cemetery.

Whilst it weathered many setbacks, the town of Murrurundi survived the great drought of 1902 and the loss of many of its young men who went to fight in the Boer War. Two of Charles' sons, Percy and Charles, and James Jnr's son, Ernest, went to serve in South Africa. Ernest died on service in 1901, Percy returned home and Charles remained, settling and marrying Bertha Pycroft in Port Elizabeth in 1906.

Murrurundi had a boost in its fortunes through the shale oil industry between 1911 and 1914. The town became a service centre after World War 1, and today it benefits from the pastoral industry, especially through horse, sheep and beef studs as well as beef and crop production. James might have been surprised to know that his town had not expanded greatly from his time and that its population is now around 800. The bark and slab huts have gone and many main street businesses of his time have disappeared. A range of moderate housing spreads over several blocks on either side of the New England Highway for a kilometre. Many shops are closed and town–based employment is weak. Parks and cultural amenities entice travellers on the Highway. Its functions remain similar to those of the time of James –catering for those journeying north or south and supplying support for its district and surrounding rural enterprises. The Pages River still has erratic flows and the level of the river is normally low. Flooding is almost unknown.

Murrurundi shared the fate of many NSW rural private and government towns, which had sound prospects for growth in the 19th century. Most withered and became small villages. Their economic conditions and town services did not match early optimism for both decentralisation and a strong rural network of growing townships throughout the colony. Centralisation, urbanisation, transport changes, and industrialisation have meant that such optimism would never be realised. In his last years, James may have sensed that his town was unlikely to be a bustling township and that its fortunes were limited.

Reprise – James and Charles

James and Charles, while experiencing the rupturing of their past together with the physical and emotional traumas of departing and arriving, settled and finally encountered conditions allowing them to pursue a livelihood and to raise a family. They moved forward. Their undoubted stress of relocation appeared to be managed. Their actions suggest they never let sorrow and regret divert them from their respective pathways, which featured elements of risk-taking together with a firm resolve. As exiles, there was no evidence that either of them wished to return to their native countries. They gained footholds in societies which generated a number of settlement problems including housing, acceptance, finance and community life. And they both had the strength and toughness of character to surmount these problems. Both would have had other notions about how their lives would unfold. And what eventuated was perhaps never in their wildest dreams.

Any consideration of James Juchau will generate speculation about his views about forced emigration, the convict experience and his subsequent journey in colonial rural NSW. He shared with other emancipists common conditions and experiences. Commitment, effort and luck enabled a second start in life. And this was better than anything he could have achieved in England. His endeavours, along with other emancipists, made positive contributions to the social and economic development of Australia.

The records show that James capitalised on his training at Carters' Barracks and secured his Certificate of Freedom without a hitch. His pioneering achievements in

Murrurundi are praiseworthy given his antecedence. He may have been fortunate that he developed links with a town founder, Thomas Haydon, who gave opportunities to James to work and invest. Outwardly the convict experience did not hinder. He pushed aside barriers and laid down the foundations for a good life for his family and his community, and he made efforts to continue links with his homeland, even though he could have resented his sentence at the Old Bailey and subsequent treatment.

We will never know his private thoughts about the events that overwhelmed his early life. Did he bear a continuing feeling of injustice as well as resenting the loss of family in England? What were the elements that brought him to focus positively on life after being emancipated? Did he ever think that out of adversity the chance to live a full and rewarding life was possible? What were his views on his life in NSW and what did he convey to his relatives when he made his trip back to London? Did he have knowledge of his Huguenot forbear, Charles, who, like him was forced to leave his country of birth and secure a new life abroad.

Outwardly James bore no grudge and grasped the opportunities colonial NSW generated. How typical was it for a juvenile convict in NSW or Tasmania to emerge from the convict experience and pursue a successful business, civic and family life? Perhaps it was not unusual given that the colonial environment was presenting a host of opportunities to profitably pioneer from rural ventures. Personal industry and astuteness as well as acquisitive strategies, sustained by supportive families, became the hallmarks of the colonialists that secured success. And James was a beneficiary first of the reformatory system and second of convict assignment. The system gave him a trade and an education. Assignment and experiences on the Scott's estate, among other things, fostered self-reliance, and gave him opportunities to realise his training and skills. The discipline, commercial insights, networks and connections gained on assignment assisted his journey to becoming a self-sustaining colonialist.

Perhaps James' story is testimony to the heartening experiences of people who, in a free society, can create a pathway to survival and success through positive and enduring deeds, which outweigh the impact any of personal adverse antecedences.

James may have agreed with a TV comment in 2013 by journalist Nick Cater about Australia: –

> *"No one comes to Australia for an easy time, they come here for a future. They do not seek deliverance, they seek the opportunity to deliver. This is not the promised land or the island of the blessed, but it is a land of promise that offers the chance of redemption".*

The experience of James in the colony of NSW prompts reflections about how a colony, created to address British social and political problems and to further the interests of its empire, became a successful vehicle of human transformation. The convicted, the troubled, the poor, and the illiterate joined with free settlers to forge a society which succeeded. Many of the transforming elements resided in the drive and ambition of individuals, who extracted much from the land, and from the relative absence of institutional, cultural and class shackles and barriers. The conjunction of aspiration and opportunity afforded by the colony together with its evolving and localising governance provisions opened a pathway to success.

Would James have been justly proud of his descendants who, in their own small way, have contributed to Australia whether through family life, service in the armed forces or service in government, the professions, the arts and business? On his 200th birthday, June 2014, he would see that many Juchaus in Australia are proud of their forbear, who overcame numerous obstacles to pioneer a successful life in Australia.

It is over 250 years since the death of Charles, the French Huguenot refugee. He could never have envisaged the pathway that a descendant great grandson, James, took in England and NSW. In a sense, he could well have understood, in the England of his time, that social, political, religious or economic turmoil could recur and that his descendants might have to face emigration challenges. He could have understandably believed that, with empires and colonies expanding, some of his descendants might have found themselves seeking their fortunes elsewhere.

Charles followed a life typical of refugees from France. Poitou under Louis XIV had given him few options for building a harmonious and free life. The web of decrees, the coercing, the destruction, mistreatment and discrimination were migration propellants boosted by the economic perils, following severe winters. In a sense he was cornered, and an appealing way out was to take the exit pathway. He, like his fellow Huguenots, entered a somewhat welcoming but challenging realm of a transforming London. His Poitou was his history. It possibly became part of his historical refrain when recounting his life stories to his family in London.

Trying to cast Charles in some character profile is difficult. We have nothing from which we can safely infer about his persona. On the basis of his deeds he was venturesome and determined. He surmounted challenges and had the confidence to undertake the task of building a new family in an alien setting.

Positive Huguenot traits and values are often romanticised and descendants of Huguenots are often claimed to possess them. Perhaps Charles possessed some of these. His financial circumstances perhaps robbed him of an opportunity to prosper in a turbulent and trying London. He may have been unsurprised that most of his descendants never emerged from the poverty trap so evident in 19th century London.

Did Charles see emigration as purely a temporary and transitory move? How did Charles view the loss of the cultural connections of home and the pressures to deemphasise his French identity? Did he believe that come what may he was to be a Londoner? Was Charles fortunate to select London as his sanctuary? Other European destinations of Huguenots generally accepted them in their midst and, for the most part, Huguenots had the opportunity to shape their migration to make new lives for themselves. A pluralistic and transforming London, stirred on by growing trade, industry and commerce, was to be a logical place for refuge for the poor and the oppressed. Charles secured housing and employment and there were sufficient economic cues in London to give confidence to Charles to build a family. London gave a safe haven, but for the poor refugees, there were continuing institutional, social and economic barriers denying a wealthier and more comfortable life. In the end his choices were limited and, given the conditions of France, safety and security were perhaps all he prayed for and needed.

***

Charles and James in their own ways successfully navigated their way into new lives in new homelands. While the circumstances of their leaving were different, they shared a common experience of settling and building a family from very limited resources. They encountered quite different passages of travel and different communities to negotiate their lives. They both sought security for raising their families and relied on their wits and energies to surmount the social and economic hurdles their host homelands presented. Without diaries and correspondence, it is not possible to know their perceptions about themselves and their host countries.

Both displayed resilience and courage to win a new life. It is worth speculating how each would have unpacked their life stories in their biographies. How did they cope with the uncertainty and fear their journeys would have generated? Both had varied and colourful backgrounds in their early rites of passage before their final settlement. Perhaps Charles would have dwelt on his exit experience and the process on adjustment in London. James is a difficult one to speculate about. It would have hinged on what he was prepared to disclose about England and the convict period. Certainly in making his way in NSW following emancipation, he would have treasured life in Murrurundi. It would have been intriguing to know how he accounted for his arrival in the colony. Did his children ever know the full story about his life as a felon and convict?

James and Charles were remarkable men forging new lives from difficult conditions. Truly the Huguenot motto, *Light after Darkness* or, as expressed in Latin, *Post Tenebras Lux*, holds for them.

Further Reading and Acknowledgements

Various histories and archives were used to give these accounts of Charles and James.

Important French histories of Poitou and the Huguenots include the following books: Mac Holt, *The French Wars of Religion, 1562-1629*, (2005); Jacques Marcade, *Protestants Poitevin de la Révocation à la Révolution*,(1998); Yves Krumenacker, *Les Protestants Du Poitou au XVIII Siècle 1681-1789*,(1998); Andre Benoist, *Paysans du Sud – Deux – Sèvres XVII-XVIII Siècle*,(2005); Michel Richard, *La Vie Quotienne des Protestants Sous L'Ancien Régime*, (1966); and Henri Dubief & Jacques Poujol, *La France Protestante*,(2005). Huguenot archives in Niort and La Couarde gave great insight into household demography, social composition and Huguenot movements. Of special importance in these archives is the work of Pastor Jean Rivierre (1904-1992), who compiled a hand written dictionary of Protestant families of historic Poitou. The work is in four volumes and is titled *Dictionnaire Alphabétique des Familles Protestants en Poitou*. My thanks also to Professor Marcade for his helpful assistance and for permission to use material from his books.

On London I found the following very helpful: Roy Porter, *London, A Social History*,(2000); Robyn Gwynn, *Huguenot Heritage*, (2001); Judith Flanders, *The Victorian City*, (2013); Lucy Inglis, *Georgian London*,(2014); and Dorothy George, *London Life In the Eighteen Century*, (1984). The library collection of the Huguenot Society in London gave important details of the Huguenot experience.

NSW colonial history has benefited from wonderful convict and settlement archives and extensive text literature in the NSW State Library, the Royal Australian Historical Society and the Shire libraries of the Upper Hunter. The Haydon papers in the University of Newcastle Library archive were most useful as were early issues of the *Maitland Mercury*. Books that proved important included: Stephen Nicholas (ed.), *Convict Workers*, (1988); Grace Karskens, *The Colony*, (2010); and Robert Hughes, *The Fatal Shore*, (1987). Special acknowledgement is given to Kerin Gorton's PhD thesis (Newcastle, 2002), *Carter's Barracks and Point Puer: The Confinement Experience of Convict Boys in Colonial Australia, 1820-1850*. The thesis has good references to the juvenile penal systems in Georgian Britain, colonial NSW and Tasmania.

My brother Hugh Juchau (Orange, NSW), and distant cousin, the late Clyde Juchau (Logan, Utah), have done much to build the Juchau genealogies and chronicles and to them I am deeply indebted. Accounts of James Juchau and his life can be found in my small monograph on James, *It Fell In to My Bag-I Landed On My Feet*, (2004) and also in *A New Tapestry: Australian Huguenot Families,* (2015). I am also indebted the various Juchaults in Poitou who gave assistance during my research visits to France. The expert assistance of Dr. Anne-Maree Whittaker, who gave guidance on the colonial archive of NSW, and Robert Nash of the Australian Huguenot Society are gratefully acknowledged. I am also indebted to my wife, Madeleine, who provided French translations and editorial assistance and the work of Evan Shapiro and his publishing company, Cilento Publishing.

Appendix
Portraying the Lives of Forbears

Writing accounts of forbears is a worthy task. Knowledge of roots and linkages not only serves the interests of descendants, it also enriches the canvas of history by illuminating the pathways of individuals who have had to navigate their lives in communities impacted by micro and macro events which constitute histories.

In writing this account of Charles and James, I continued to be unsettled because my portrayals could not secure personal accounts of their lives. I continued to imagine how they coped and what conversations they had with those who were part of their journeys through life. I wanted to hear their voices and to understand how they interpreted and reacted, as well as to know what was in their characters to enable them to emerge from the darkness of their pasts.

Whilst understanding that imagination and research give historic characters of movies and plays an extensive dialogue with the full range of emotions I nevertheless get annoyed by the certainty and authority most of these performances portray. Witness reports of occurrences can lend authenticity to portrayals, but still fall short because I want the human encounters of main characters to be faithful. And I know this can never be.

While writing these accounts I wanted to text or phone Charles and James to get feedback on their feelings and coping mechanisms. In a way, I felt that I had betrayed them because I ventured my own views on how they coped. I know I was shadow boxing in the dark, as I attempted to explain how, under known events and adverse situations, they managed to survive.

Historical family biographies will never capture faithfully the human aspect of the lives of forbears. Archived correspondence can give occasional helpful hints. I am envious of those whose families who can access a rich and extensive correspondence to assist their family history endeavours.

About the Author

The writer is a direct descendant of Charles Juchau (1690-1756). He is the great, great grandson of James Thomas Juchau (1814-1897). His great grandfather was Charles Francis Juchau (1844-1923), his grandfather Clarence Louis Juchau (1888-1965) and father Hugh Louis Juchau (1916-1985).

He is an Emeritus Professor of Western Sydney University where he retired in 2007. He was a financial educator and is a writer and consultant. He has lived and worked in the Pacific, New Zealand, Britain and USA. His writing has appeared in journals, texts and monographs.

Outside family, travel, writing, golf and horse racing Roger's current interests are researching early NSW and Huguenot histories.

Roger Hugh Juchau (1941 –) lives in Balmain and Wallaga Lake, NSW.